DIMENSIONS
of
Harlan Ellison®

Edited by Jason Davis

AN **E** OFFERING

EDGEWORKS
ABBEY

To order definitive Ellison books, visit
www.HarlanEllisonBooks.com

Assistant Editor: Cynthia Davis

ISBN: 978-1-946542-02-1

FIRST EDITION

Thanks to Bo Nash & Tim Richmond.

Special Thanks to Jeffrey Cochrane & Scott V. Norris,
who were invaluable in assembling this book.

Copyright acknowledgements appear on pages 141–142,
which constitutes an extension of this copyright page.

CONTENTS

NOTA BENE

The contents of this volume were written between 1951 and 1955, when Harlan Ellison was between the ages of 17 and 22. Though these pieces were written prior to the sale of "Glowworm" to Larry Shaw of *Infinity*, a number of stories written toward the end of this period—"Gnomebody," "Life Hutch," "Night Vigil," "The Silver Corridor," and "Who Wilts the Lettuce?," to name a few—were among his earliest sales.

For years, Ellison refused to allow material from this amateur phase of his career to be reprinted—relenting a few times for THE ESSENTIAL ELLISON, the *Rabbit Hole*, and ROUGH BEASTS— but the advent of the Harlan Ellison Books Preservation Project finally provided a perfect venue for this act of literary archæology, and H. E. relented with his oft-proffered quote that, "At least doctors get to bury their mistakes."

On Harlan's behalf, I ask you to remember the context in which the works were written and published, and cut the kid some slack; he turned out to be one hell of a writer.

JASON DAVIS

Green Denouement
16 March 1952

Strange and wonderful are the secrets the jungle jealously
guards. Secrets Man has been unable to fathom.
Thomas Brockman
HISTORY OF THE COLONIZATION
OF JUNGLE-COVERED PLANETS

A shimmering blue fog sprang up from the jungle as though by
magic. The animals deep within the mass's entwined bowels screamed
rhythmically.

From somewhere there came a rumble.

And then the rocket sped overhead.

It banked rapidly and disappeared over the horizon. Within an
hour it again zoomed into view. It slowed and stalled, tube flames
sputtering consumptively, and rushed toward the fringe of the jungle.

With a short burst of its motors, it settled onto the plain, leaving a
line of burnt out brush and Kopi-trees.

It settled quickly, save the cracking and popping of its tubes, into
its own private trough; a depression six feet deep that had not been
there before.

The rocket opened.

Man had come to Bootes IV.

"**D**amn jungle blood-bugs," spat Thorstern.

He swatted ineffectually at the cluster of winged slate-gray bugs that had gathered on his left leg. They dispersed for a moment and returned when he took his hand away.

Where they had lit, a welt arose and Thorstern began to scratch frantically, cursing in both languages he had learned at Space Academy.

the jungle nodded approvingly

Volzer, the captain of the Planetary Exploration and Exploitation Survey ship number PEES t-M09, stuck a blade of the saw-grass into his mouth and leaned back against the thick trunk of a Kopi-tree.

"Too bad we have that full time recorder in the ship," he mumbled, brushing a blood-bug off the tip of his nose, "if that thing didn't work all the seven months we're out, we could fake up some kind of report and go home.

"But no, that damned thing's gotta have a report every day of the Germination Period. So we waste our young lives away here and each day at 0080 say, 'No report.'"

The other three men acquiesced silently.

the jungle grew flustered and removed
the source of their discomfort

"Say," marveled Fellinger, "notice the blood-bugs have disappeared?"

"Yeah, that *is* strange. This planet ain't quite so bad without 'em," said the pile-room man, Narkey.

"I still don't like it. This heat...and all this jungle. I don't like the idea of staying here two more months. This place isn't what you'd call a summer resort." It was Volzer speaking.

the jungle realized a crisis was at hand
and decided to strike

Suddenly the very jungle seemed to come to life. Right before their eyes, the floor of the jungle-like plain, which, they had found, was made of a carpet of thick, intertwined Kopi-leaves, rose and split up into the mass and disappeared within the leafy fronds.

They leaped to their feet...and were swallowed up.

Green swam before their eyes.

Green everywhere they looked. They seemed to be staring as through a membrane over which ran a stream of sticky green fluid.

Before them the rocket swam into view. It was surrounded by more of the membranous mists.

the jungle felt odd

With a whup like the popping of a paper bag, the four spacemen and the ship were ejected. They landed on the grassy plain which began to unmercifully jostle and bounce them till they ran to the ship which was hopping frantically around on its side under the movements of the gyrating ground.

They got into their ship and took off.

the jungle sighed contentedly

"Whewwww," Johnney Narkey let out a long and thoroughly expressive sigh.

"What in the devil happened?" It was Fellinger.

"That was a man-eating planet. The whole thing. It swallowed the ship and us and then began digesting the lot of us," the words tumbled out of Thorstern's mouth in a way that showed the effects had not worn off, even thousands of miles away from the planet.

"We'd better radio back to Terra and warn them to send out a destroyer fleet and burn that trap out of the void," Fellinger advised.

Captain Volzer, silent till then, spoke up quietly, "I don't think that will be necessary, Gentlemen."

They stared for a moment and then in outrage yelled, "Yeah? Well, look what it did to *us*! That thing was hungry! And it'll do it to other humans."

"As a matter of fact," said the captain, "I don't think it will. We keep hearing of the superiority of humanity all the time. Man is at the apex of life. It's drummed into our heads. Our 'manifest destiny.' But we've just received the biggest insult of our lives, Gentlemen. That jungle vomited us up."

Luna

30 March 1952

And now art thou cursed from the Earth, which hath
opened her mouth to receive thy brother's blood from
thy hand...

GENESIS IV:11

Mrs. MacDonald had always wanted twins.

And now the house of MacDonald was blessed with the wails of
dual throats screaming for food at the same time.

That was the second thing you noticed about the twins; their too
serious competition. The first thing you noticed was the comparison
between their hair. They were exact twins save the fact that one had
off-color rust-red hair and the other's was blond.

In more than one way that was their *only* difference.

For the MacDonald twins, by the very fact that they *were* twins,
had to compete. Not against outsiders as normal youngsters would,
but against each other in a deadly do-or-die fight that was at times
highly entertaining.

They fought to get the first bowl of Pablum.

A quarrel started over possession of the two-wheeler.

At the age of twenty, the trouble began over the football queen.

One night at dinner, the boy they called "Red" announced he was
entering the Air Force.

The next night "Bud" announced the same intention.

Clearing his throat, the General sent a withering glance down the
table. It served its purpose. The second lieutenant who had, a moment
before, been whispering, embarrassedly closed his mouth.

Once more ridding himself of annoying phlegm, the white-
mustached commander began, "Well, gentlemen, it's come."

He consulted the sheaf of neatly stacked papers before him and
then stroked the slightly flabby contour of his chin, a sign of officer's
barracks cooking, in a movement that showed obvious concern.

"Although it isn't necessary, I should like to take a moment to review the three years we have spent here at Alamogordo. To heighten and point up...rather than remind you, of the things that have happened here. Then I shall ask you to make a decision.

"Three years ago we learned that not only was space flight possible, but that Russia was hard at work upon a space satellite *and* a moon rocket. After the preliminary tests at Muroc, we were commissioned to get an American made rocket up there first...at any cost.

"They feared the Third World War then. Well, it's hard to forget but we've been engaged in that war for sixteen months.

"Gentlemen, it is only a matter of time!"

A shadow of weariness played across the General's face for a moment, washing away all the surface brusqueness he had displayed, then he continued, "We needed a man to make the trip although the rocket was near-perfect. It was discovered that the takeoff and landing could be handled more efficiently by a human than a Reinschmann Integrator.

"So the call went out. Seventeen hundred and fifty some boys and men have passed through the conditioning shelters of this base, gentlemen. From the Army, Navy, Air Corps, and specialized organizations that thought they had our man.

"Out of those seventeen hundred only two remain. And with the flight scheduled for 1200 tomorrow, we must make our choice. Both men have been thoroughly briefed."

A dapper-looking Colonel to the speaker's right said, "How is it that there are *two*? Wasn't our training program sufficient to pick the better of the two?"

"Amazingly, gentlemen, they are twin brothers. Equally matched, equally qualified. Both have high mental ratings and approximately the same physical condition. It really is quite a coincidence.

"It falls to you then, to choose the one to be the first Earth man on the Moon. Here are the reports," and he slid the sheaf of papers down the table, "You will please choose one of the MacDonald brothers."

They sat for hours examining the reports, cardiographs, training cards, and encephalographs. They scrutinized the I. Q. tests and finally decided upon the simple expedient of flipping a coin.

The General fumbled in his pocket for a moment and then came up with a piece of silver.

His thumb snapped against his index finger and the circle of metal arched upward and spiraled like a silver fish into his palm. With a fleeting motion he slapped the hand containing the coin onto his opposite palm and turned to the man next to him.

"Call it."

"Heads."

One eye stared metallically at them.

Rising above the New Mexico desert like some leviathan carved of silver, the rocket poised itself on metal fins as though waiting, half-alive, to spring into the darkening night.

Beneath its stately bulk, the myriad tasks of preparation were being carried out by the ant-like figures who swarmed madly about, while the Needle, imperious and disinterested in their maneuvers looked toward the star-flecked sky.

On the scaffolding leading upward around the tapering hull, the interspersed flashes of welders' torches made for a distinctive display of color. But, to the assembled group of scientists and army personnel gathered next to the lift, the display was wasted.

They stood and watched the almost identical twins who conversed in low tones, apart from their group.

Clothed in a garment of clinging metallic substance, the twin with flaming red hair placed one arm over the shoulder of his towhead brother and silently gazed beyond him to the quiet mountains which loomed giantly behind the base.

"Red" MacDonald drew in a breath between his teeth to the accompaniment of a soft whistling sound and said almost inaudibly, "Well, I guess this is it, 'Buddy.'"

His brother nodded silently although a trace of a Mona Lisa-ish smile played across his lips.

"Yeah, this is it. Good luck, 'Red.'"

They shook hands and the Lieutenant with the blond hair turned and strode purposefully back toward the base post.

The other twin turned and went back to the little knot of men waiting by the lift.

He shook hands all around and then stepped onto the elevator which bore him rapidly to the dizzy heights above.

He entered the ship, sealed and dogged the port and went to the control room, passing through the many lockered storerooms.

He sank into the pneumatic couch, fastened the straps, and slid the maneuverable control box from its niche in the wall to a spot directly in front of his chest. After the process of turning and twisting numerous dials, the high keening whine of the base announcer emanated from the speaker above MacDonald's head.

"Five minutes till storage port close-up. Please hurry with air tanks. We are thirteen seconds behind schedule. The storage port will be closed at 1190."

MacDonald nestled himself deeper into the padding while above him the voice droned on in an urgent tone:

"One minute and ten seconds to blastoff. Remove escalator. Seal access port." A pause, then: "Port sealed. Prepare for blastoff. Will all unauthorized personnel please move behind the shielding at Bunker Number Four. Will all unauthorized person..."

"Red" MacDonald let his thoughts soar outward. Past the Moon, past the Outer Planets, and the Stars. To the infinite reaches of the unknown Universe where he could become one with his thoughts, alone.

"What do you know," he half-mumbled, "I finally won out over my brother. It took twenty-three years to prove who was the better man... and now I've done it."

He didn't even feel the scaffolds slither silently away from the ship as the announcer said, "Blastoff in twenty seconds. Will all authorized personnel please retreat to the shielding by Bunker Number One. Please! This is your last warning.

"Ten seconds to Blastoff. Nine seconds."

The ship shuddered as the converters in the hold began to whine with power. The ship gave a lurch...

"Four seconds to Blastoff..."

The muted throb became a deafening roar as the watchers donned polarized glasses. Suddenly a corona-like radiance came from the tubes and with a mighty rush of power, the rocket leaped from the dry New Mexico desert like some powerful bird that had been chained to Earth.

The sliver of silver knifed upward and was soon lost to sight.

MacDonald regained consciousness with a splitting headache but pulled his senses together to scan the control box as he had been trained. Fuel: in good shape; air supply: about the same; altitude: okay...no, wait a minute. Look at the chronograph and the time sheet. This rocket was behind schedule.

Must be extra weight.

MacDonald released himself from the straps and floated through the gravityless ship to the storage room.

A half hour of searching brought him to the locker from which blood dripped from beneath the door. He threw it open.

His twin was crumpled within.

They had argued back and forth for hours. "Red" MacDonald argued that the method of selection was wrong. "Red" yelled at the top of his lungs that "Buddy" was a crazy maniac, and that it would kill him.

It dawned on both of them at approximately the same time that they might very well *both* be killed. There was only so much fuel, to carry so much weight. The extra person put in another hundred and seventy-odd pounds. And while they might get to the moon, and perhaps even take off again, they certainly would be too short of fuel to make a safe landing back on Earth.

And as for air. Short there too.

And food...

Both the brothers kept the knowledge to himself.

The moon, Luna, grew bloated in the ports.

Soon they could feel the small, almost unnoticeable pull of the Moon's one-sixth Earth gravity.

Then they landed.

They came down in the center of Aristotle amid a puff of rock pumice and moon-dust that had lain undisturbed for eons. There was a spare spacesuit in the rocket, so they came out at the same time.

They came out onto the face of the Earth's satellite. Onto the dead and airless plain that was covered with the burst bubbles that formed craters, mute evidence of days long gone, when the moon had been molten.

They both clasped the flagstaff tightly in their heated gloves and mumbled into the inter-suit receivers. "I, the first man on the Moon, take this planet in the name of God and the United States."

Then the blond-haired MacDonald boy turned to the horizon above which floated the globe of the Earth and said, "Up there they've been killing each other off, ruining the Eden they might have had. But here there will be no evil. Here there..."

He never finished his statement.

His brother stood over his fallen body, the helmet, cracked and devoid of air, surrounding a queerly crimson head. A bloody rock gripped firmly in his mitten.

...and Cain MacDonald walked slowly back to the rocket while behind him, lying in a pool of his own life-blood, was his brother Abel.

Trapping the Beast
30 March 1952

ABOUT THIS STORY *AND* THIS INTRODUCTION: Basically, this thing should NOT have been published. It is against my better judgement that it *is*. In the first place because it was merely a letter written from myself to Stephen F. Schultheis of Warren, Ohio, a fellow s-f fan and strictly in fun and in the second place because too many people outside the CSFS won't know what in the heck it is about. Or what makes it (as Schultheis terms it) "so blasted funny." [EDITOR'S NOTE: Schultheis was the president of the Cleveland Science Fiction Society, the aforementioned CSFS.]

For those who won't understand without an explanation of the story *AND* that more-confusing-than-ever introduction, this is dedicated. [E.N.: Schultheis's lengthy introductory note, which diagnosed Ellison as suffering from "that peculiar form of mental decay known as bibliomania—bibliomania literatura fantastica, to be exact" has not been reprinted here.]

Harlan Ellison has at times had quite a few arguments with the aforementioned Schultheis. On one occasion at a rather disreputable bookshop on the west side of Cleveland, Stephen F. grabbed a copy of John Taine's BEFORE THE DAWN (an extremely rare volume) from 'neath the questing digits of the "Mighty Moron" Ellison.

On a later occasion, Ellison was warned that if he came to New Orleans for the Annual Science Fiction Convention, the rest of the fen from Cleveland would disembark from any bus he would enter.

That then is the framework from which the rather subtle (like a sledge-hammer) bit of humor following has been derived. We certainly hope you like it because WE certainly don't intend to turn the page on which "The Monster" begins. You're on your own...

HARLAN ELLISON®
Editor, the *CSFS Bulletin*

I

Seventy million miles from the Solar System was a planet.

It was a hot and steamy planet.

In the thick, living jungles of the planet was a beast.

The planet was known to galactic observers as Warrum, and was the home of the horribly fat and bloated monster known as the Steevthyse.

It was a slovenly thing that wore a skin of a sheen resembling nickel, but loose and plastic-like, as a transparent raincoat might be. It had two appendages, leathery things that resembled respectively a suitcase and a briefcase. Rough comparisons, you understand.

II

And speeding through the cathedral of Space there was a sliver of silver metal. A space ship.

Within the space ship there was but one man. Captain Harl Eller. It was his assignment to capture the horrible monster of Warrum, and bring it and its booty back to Terra.

Eller was grim. Grim and determined. The task ahead was no mean objective. To separate the Steevthyse from its horde and capture it was a task that had been set before many another agent of the Galactic Orderlies Operational Police.

Each time a GOOP officer had been sent to Warrum to capture it, all that had been heard was a static-filled message to the effect that, "There ain't no book shops down here!"

So now he, Harl Eller, had been selected.

Grim, thought Eller, that *he* of all the agents should finally get the job. He had had a run-in with the Steevthyse once before. It was several eons back, he remembered.

He let his mind wander.

Wandering mind...

III

The book shop of Syrtis Straight Flush was just ahead.

Harl quickened his step.

Suddenly from a public air-omni that bore the large dirt-smudged legend of See-Tee-Urps, burst a horribly sluggish animal that was never meant for the speed it was now striving to attain.

It leaped for the book shop door, its two tentacle-like appendages quivering slightly. The one resembling a battered suitcase slapped at the plastilite door, and it was inside.

Harl, sensing danger, cautiously followed, noting that the place was a disreputable hole. "Just the kind of dump you'd expect to see THAT thing in," he muttered.

The floor was unswept, the windows were clouded over, and the neontube in the ceiling cast but a malefic shadow of its former brilliance.

On the wall was a sign that said dirtily:

ALL MAGAZINES 25¢

Even through the dirt, Harl was elated. Only a quarter for all those old Gernsbeans *Thunders* in that pile. What a find!

The owner was as disreputable as his place. A slob. He stood behind a glass case (broken-fronted) and leered at a pair of booby-soxers who were tearing through a pile of comixxes, while he wound the propeller of a little model of an antique air-flivver up tight.

With a swish of his good arm (he had a hook...equipped with a coin changer on the other) he released the plane. It sailed over the room and just missed striking Harl in the head.

In a flash he had his Atom-Birdbath-Chickenfat-BEM-Splash-

Disintigo Ray out, and had blasted away half the front wall in a wild shot at the madly careening air-flivver.

The owner, not the least bit perturbed about the store front, continued to leer at the commixx-gazers.

Then Harl spotted them.

On a small shelf, on the other side of the store, was a group of, not magazines, not commixxes, but books! Yes, books.

Books that had been banned and obsolete lo these fifty years. A real live breathing, living book. And then he spotted *it*!

The brown backing said:

After the Dusk
by Jan Paine

He lurched forward, almost drunkenly.

But a briefcase came from nowhere, and whisked the treasure from under his questing fingers.

The monster, which he identified from memories of WANTED signs in the post office as the monster of Warrum, the Steevthyse, ran (or rather slopped) over to the owner of the shop and said in a rasping, cunning, squeezing voice, "'ow much?"

"Five hundred thousand credits," wheezed the owner.

"Fi..." gasped Harl, almost unintelligibly.

"I can pay," chortled the monster, peeling off a small stack of hundred thousand credit notes.

"I don't like to argue with customers," sneered the owner at Harl, who just gaped, "The second time they come in, I just tell 'em we're all out of magazines. I don't hafta argue."

"But I was about to take that book myself!" stormed Harl, his anger rising.

"Too bad," giggled the monster, edging toward the portway.

With a heave he was gone, out the portway and into an air-omni that bore the legend, NEWORLEONNO OMNI.

From a window the monster's head appeared as he yelled, "No use chasing me. If you get on this bus, I'll get off. And so will all my friends. So you'd better not show your face on it."

And then the Omni roared out of sight.

IV

The rocket settled to the thick, matted floor of the jungle of Warrum. Harl donned an atmo-suit, and stalked from the port, the remembrance of the Syrtis Straight Flush Book Shop incident still hot in his mind.

Hardly armed, but wanting to take the monster single-handed, he shifted his pack containing the Denning atom-slammer rifle, the Greeley grenades, the BEM-blotter, the Felascoo disintegrator, the Rayle-ray, the Hanlin-flamer, and the Davidson offset-vari-harpsichord amplifier thought deadener, to the small atom-cannon mounted half-track; and set out, the disintegrator robots following behind, dragging the missile-launchers.

Up a short hill, down through a vine-covered depress, and then...

The fortress stood in the middle of a huge moat of quicksand.

Harl Eller swung a thin neo-plast rope from his utility leg (wooden) and, releasing the trigger mechanism, shot it across the moat till it caught on a sharp, protruding corner of the fortress. Anchoring it, Harl climbed hand over hand to the fortress. It was not until he had thrown one leg (flesh) over the cornice, that he realized the rope was not caught on a buttress of the fort, but the buttress of the Steevthyse.

His nose.

"Ugh," winced Harl, "what a slovenly nose. In fact, what a slovenly beast."

And then they were at it with hand blasters and tongs.

The air ossified and odorized, it coagulated and congealed, it froze and frothed, it bubbled and burst.

And in the end, but one remained, clutching a book that said on the brown jacket:

AFTER THE DUSK
by
Dr. Heric Church Buzzer

It was Harl Eller.

And the moral is: IF YOU'VE GOT TO LIVE IN A FORTRESS, DON'T HAVE A LONG NOSE!

The Beer Campaign
as by Michael Frazier, April 1952

"Where did you say you were from?"

"Mars."

"That's what I thought you said."

Silence

"Let's take it again, Mister, slower this time."

The little man with the unusually ruddy complexion stood before the befuddled brewer, shifting from one foot to another, till gathering his breath into what appeared to be the most sunken of chests, he began for the second time. "We want beer for our canals.

"Our canals are dry—we want beer for them. Is that clear?"

Wide-eyed, the beer-blender stammered in acquiescence, "Yeah, yeah, it's clear. But I don't unnerstan'. You better see Mister Blowzer."

He motioned toward a door at the rear of the fermenting room. "Right through there," he instructed, "back through the hall till you come to the door leading to the main offices. Tell the girl at the desk you wanta see Mister Blowzer."

The little crimson-hued man thanked the brewmaster in an absent-minded way and went swiftly through the designated orifice.

Behind him, the brewer was standing wiping his sweaty forehead and mumbling something to the effect that they ought to put better padlocks on the fermenting room doors. All kinds of screwlooses were getting in.

Winding his way through the hall toward the office, the little man kept staring straight ahead, as though he were worrying about matters of great import. Like the salvation of a race.

He was.

He entered the reception room of the Blowzer Beer Company and walked quietly across the deeply carpeted floor to the reception desk behind which a bleached blonde sat improving her education with a copy of *Mad Love Escapades* combined with *Torrid Passion Affairs* magazine.

"A-hemmm."

The gum stopped moving, the eyes unglazed, the magazine lowered, and the pseudo-blonde head swivelled.

"Yes?" Extremely nasal.

"I would like to see Mister Blowzer."

"Who shall I say is calling," the girl almost yawned and took out a pencil.

"Mister Tzzyzzl."

"Eh...?"

"Uh...just say Mister...er...Smith is here."

She gave him a peculiar, sidelong glance, and raising her heavily perfumed body from her reception chair, edged away toward a paneled door near the back of the room, behind a wooden entrance gate.

In a few moments the girl came out again and said, "Mister Blowzer will see you. Won't you go r-right in." But she didn't open the gate as was her usual wont.

The little man went through the gate and into the office and presence of H. Herman Blowzer III.

Imagine a bottle of Blowzer's Fabulous Beer. The round, almost bloated-looking body; the thick neck of the bottle, the brownish hue of the glass. Just picture what a bottle of that beer would look like with a pair of fat arms and blubbery legs added and with a lumpish head plopped on top.

H. Herman Blowzer III.

"Something I can do for you my good fellow," wheezed the bloated lump of protoplasm behind the desk.

"We saw your advertisement," answered the reddish-hued man matter-of-factly.

"What ad...oh, you must mean our new one. Yes, a clever bit of advertising if I must say so myself." He added confidentially, "I thought of it myself. Rather ingenious, ay? Most beer advertisements say their beer is the best in the city; or the state; or the country; or once in a while even the continent. But MY ad says that "Blowzer Beer is the best on the entire planet Earth."

He added reflectively, lost in his own mood, "Deucedly clever of me I should say. Did I tell you I thought of it?"

"We saw your ad."

"Yes, I know. You said that."

"We would like to order some beer."

"Well, well, that's fine," chortled Blowzer, reaching into his desk drawer for a pencil and order blank. "I don't often take orders myself anymore, but since you're here..." He left the sentence unfinished having noticed that his guest was not paying the least bit of attention, "Now how much of an order would you like to place?"

"Fifty trillion barrels a year—indefinitely."

The plop as the pencil dropped on the paper was quite distinct in the office.

Blowzer hunched forward, as much as his bulk would allow, "I don't believe I heard you rightly, Mr. Smith. What did you say?"

"Fifty trillion barrels a year—indefinitely."

The beer baron pulled an oily hankie from his suit coat pocket and swabbed at his forehead which had begun to sweat profusely. "Fif...fifty *TRILLION* barrels?" he inquired, the accent on the trillion containing a slightly hysterical note.

"That is correct."

"And where may I ask, is it going?" brazened Blowzer, sensing a joke.

"To Mars."

The significance did not sink in immediately. "In what state?"

"No state. The planet Mars."

Morgum got thrown out again. It was the third place that day he had tried. They wouldn't believe him. What was so fantastic about being from Mars?

So Earth *hadn't* been visited before. So what? Couldn't these idiots believe something when you told them? It was disconcerting to say the least. Morgum had been certain that the Blowzer Company was the one that could solve his problem. A company that had advertising on a planetwide scale must certainly be more far-sighted than the others.

But it was the same old story.

Wincing, the little red man lifted himself off the pavement and staggered dejectedly away from the brewery.

As he weaved away from the beer factory, the high metal fence suddenly swung open and out ran, if it could be called that, the bulbous Blowzer.

"Mr. Smith. Oh, Mr. Smith," he puffed and wheezed as he propelled his massive body toward Morgum, "I'm awfully sorry I was so rash. If you'll come back, I'll try to make amends."

Morgum was astounded. "Why did you change your mind? Do you mean that you believe me?"

"Certainly, certainly, my boy," he rumbled, "I was just testing your... uh...stamina, yes, that's it...your stamina."

"My socio-culturegraph never mentioned *this* custom," Morgum mused. "Will you sell us the beer now?"

"Certainly, my good fellow, all in good time. Won't you come back now and tell your story to our board of trustees. A...uh...sale of this kind needs more confirmation and...uh...explanation."

Morgum stood at the head of the long table. Down one side were twelve men. Down the other side were twelve other men. And at the head of the table facing him was H. Herman Blowzer III.

Unhesitating, Morgum Tzzyzzl began, "Mars, as your scientists have suspected, is a much older planet than yours. Her youth was several hundred thousand years ago, according to your time. But through the centuries, the planet has grown old and our lands have dried up. This is chiefly due to the fact that our "water" (actually it was a chemical equivalent of your H_2O) has evaporated. Even our technology, far in advance of yours, could not regain enough of the lost moisture to refertilize the ground. Our canals dried out and we began to die off.

"Naturally we worried about the problem, but being a race much like yourselves, the average person did not care and went about their work and play without a thought to the future.

"Now the situation is serious."

He stopped momentarily as if gathering his thoughts, and then once again plunged on, "Within the last fifty years, though, the situation has become so bad that we knew we must do something or eventually perish.

"Although we had space travel many years ago, we were so content on Mars that we never bothered to visit you. Till a half a century ago it was suggested that perhaps you Earthmen might help us."

The men around the table looked startled. Up till then, they had listened as to a child telling a fairy tale, but now they came suddenly awake.

Morgum continued, "I was delegated to come to Earth and try to establish a trade system to obtain what we need for something we might have that *you* would need.

"In my search around the planet, I have heard it mentioned that gold is valuable. Also pitchblende. We have great deposits of these metals which, frankly, we consider useless. But if you can make use of them, we would be more than happy to strike a bargain."

The twenty-five trustees, Blowzer included, looked at each other. "One thing though," queried a bald-headed fellow from the far end of the table. "What do we have that you want so much?"

"Beer."

Incredulity ruled.

"What?"

"Beer? Is he crazy?"

"What is this? A joke?"

"A hoax?"

"...out of his mind!"

"Gentlemen, gentlemen," Blowzer turned red, as red as Morgum, and bellowed at the top of his lungs at the raging trustees, "Please let Mr. Yzzy...er...Tyzz...uh...Smith, finish."

As soon as comparative silence had fallen, Morgum began once again, where he had left off, "The chemical properties of 3.2 beer are conducive to good growth in our plant life. The malt and hops, fermented and combined with the components, we have found, provide the necessary chemicals in the right amounts to not only rejuvenate the flora of our planet, but make it strong and healthy. And besides, Martians LIKE beer."

Again pandemonium reigned.

"If you like it so much and it helps the flowers, or whatever, why don't you make some yourself?" It was the same trustee as before.

Calmly the red Martian answered, "We find that not only don't we have enough plant life to make beer, but somehow, in the advancement of our culture, we neglected to learn how to brew it at all. The only beer we have is what we buy here on Earth and TP back to Mars for experiment."

"'You do *what* with the beer?"

"TP it."

"What in the heck is TP?"

"Teleport. That is how we would get the beer to Mars that we bought from you."

This time it seemed as though the walls would crash about their ears. Every member of the trustee board had chosen sides. Some were screaming invectives at Blowzer and some were screaming ditto at Tzzyzzl.

Finally Blowzer again stilled them, by whanging and banging on the table with a wooden mallet till the thing snapped off at the neck.

"Now shut up," he bellowed, again crimsoning like the Martian, "Uh...Mr. Smith, would you mind retiring to the foyer till I take this up with the boys...that is, the board.

It was a statement, not a question.

Morgum retired.

As soon as the heavy door closed behind the tiny red man Hell broke loose once more. Till Blowzer stilled the waves of protest. All but Baldy.

"What do you mean getting us all the way from our work to come here and listen to this, this—" he fumbled for the word, "screwball."

Another chimed in, "What kind of a hoax are you pulling this time Blowzer?"

With a raise of a beefy hand, Blowzer motioned them into silence. He then simply stated, "He is undoubtedly a crackpot...but can you see the advertising?"

They could.

The advertising screamed:

FIRST IN MILWAUKEE

THEN IN WISCONSIN

NEXT IN THE UNITED STATES

FOLLOWED BY THE NORTH AMERICAN CONTINENT

AND THEN THE WHOLE EARTH

BUT NOW...

BLOWZER'S FABULOUS BEER IS SOLD

...ON MARS!!!

The radios and tv sets were loaded with the Blowzer ads. Soon the whole country was singing the Blowzer jingle:

Blowzer Beer the frothy drink
    With it make your glasses clink.
Sold in Milwaukee, New York too...
    Mars says Blowzer is best for you.

GABRIEL HEATTER:
Ah yes, folks, there is unusual news ton-n-n-night. It is more than rumored that Herman Blowzer, of the beer company of the same

name, has not only made contact with a real Martian, but is selling him a fabulous amount of beer to fill his canals. The beer is to be shipped via a new method. Teleportation. It is said that the Martia...

WALTER WINCHELL:
Dit-da-dit-dit-dit...
Good evening Mr. and Mrs. North America and all the ships at sea. FLASH! Although the international situation is still grave, the spotlight is still focused upon Milwaukee, Wisconsin in the U. S. For there the first "interplanetary meeting" is taking place between H. Herman Blowzer III of the Blowzer Beer Company and an unidentified Martian. Although it is probably a hoax, it is a good advertising campaign for Blowzer Beer. So good in fact that sales have increased ninety-seven per cent. But we with common horse sense know that there is no such thing as a "Martian." And to have one buying beer...why that is just fantas...

The newspapers saw a chance for a crusade. They blazed their messages all over the planet:

BLOWZER HOAX SHAMEFUL

CHEAP PUBLICITY STUNT RAKES IN GELT

NO MARTIANS!!! IT'S ALL A FAKE!!!

But at the Blowzer beer plant a huge machine was making it difficult for the employees to park their cars. It stood in the center of the parking lot and had fifteen hundred pipes connected with it to the fermenting rooms.

It was a massive thing with protuberances all over it. And beer, fresh from the vats, was being piped through at a rate that would equal, in one year, 50,000,000,000,000 barrels!

If they *only* knew.

Also causing trouble for the workers were the stacks and stacks of bricks of gold and pitchblende on the front lawn, guarded by Brinks.

But the papers yelled:

FAKE!!!

Blowzer looked at the sales chart. It went up so high, he had to add an annex. He glanced out the window at the bricks of gold and pitchblende and shook his head. Smith, or whatever his name was, had disappeared the day after the pipes were hooked up.

Then the next day, these bricks had been out on the lawn. But he didn't worry about it too much. So the gold and pitchblende were given in return, enough for fifty years of beer at least, but that didn't mean Smith was a Martian.

Well, he wasn't going to worry about it.

Just look at that chart, will you?

Morgum hiccuped contentedly and looked down at the sparkling white foam on the stein of beer he held. He hicced again.

(NEWS ITEM) Observers at Mount Palomar have reported a strange transformation. They have noted that the heretofore dark lines on the planet Mars, which had been labeled as "canals," have suddenly changed to a sparkling, shimmery white. Those that are dark are changing rapidly and noted scientists are...

In 2003, the first rocket landed on the red planet and found...

A race of drunkards and a booming Alka-Selzer business.

The Lost Atomic
a hilarious tale of multiple worlds
April 1952

At times it is rather difficult to be a third party in the telling of a story. Especially since there is no real reason for a "third party" at all.

Suffice it to say that I know the story and if it weren't for me...you would never have come to hear it, or at least *all* of it.

I'm what you might term a "necessary evil."

Although not having been proven to the satisfaction of a great many of Earth's scientists, it is generally accepted that there is a good chance of there being other, what you might term, dimensions.

Some speak of the fourth, fifth, and seventeenth dimensions as being extensions (sometimes at right angles to ours) of the Earth here-and-now dimension.

Actually, you know, it isn't so.

They aren't like extensions at all. They are like... Well, did you ever get one of those birthday presents all wrapped up in a monstrous box? And when you opened it, there was another box somewhat smaller? And when you opened that one, another? And still another? Take that situation and add the phrase ad infinitum.

Now you know the whole story of the dimension theory.

If you will pardon me, I should like to say that I never thought I would do as fine a job of narrating as I am.

But we had best get on with it. It really caused quite a stir in Trxymmm, you know.

...or do you?

It would seem best to tell it in various time styles. For you see time is not relative in the dimensions. It may have happened last May for all you care, but it will not happen in Trxymmm till the Ourpi of Gluj.

Nonetheless...

There is a scientist (if he could be termed that) in Trxymmm whose only thought at the moment is to reach a bowl of ripe potahs on his desk.

He starts across the room (it isn't *actually* a room) to take one but en route collides with his office transtemper.

It is an accident that rarely occurs, the transtempors having been pretty well perfected by this day and age (or sluck and foouhj, if you prefer), but even so, the scientist's foot (it really isn't) collides with the floor switch and the machine, idly pointed toward the desk, casts its blue radiance over a small paperweight atomic that rests there.

With a nearly inaudible snapping sound, indicative of the closing of space where the atomic had been, it disappears.

Consternation, in assorted degrees, plays over the face (?) of the scientist as he puts through a non-relay mental beam to the police (well, you wouldn't actually call them "police," but...).

Instantly they arrive and having taken the information, shoot the scientist.

Naturally they shoot him, he made a mistake. What else *was* there to do with him?

But it is understood by all present that even if the scientist *were* alive, he could never make as big a mistake as this one.

An atomic in another dimension. The concept was staggering. The thought ghastly. The possible results horrible.

Remember what I told you about non-relative time?

Well...

They're going to call in the most talented inter-dimensional detective of them all. Tyreer-kouj. Why is he so good? Wasn't he born in a trans-temporal realigner ship between Trxymmm and Norvofass? What better environment to build up the right mental attitudes for interdimensional detecting?

They've sent out hundreds of squads already to try and find it. They realize the urgency connected with the accident. Not so much the harm it would do to the dimension it landed in, although it was sure to destroy *it*, but think of the repercussions on Tryxmmm. With the atoms of one dimension warped, the others would begin to melt in upon themselves. Tornadoes, hurricanes, tidal waves, perhaps even a lovareen or two. Good Lord (not ours, of course)!

So Tyreer-kouj is going to go out. Or went out? Sometimes even *I* get mixed up with this time business. It really is a bother, you know.

It was a faintly luminous trail of burst pen-atoms that kouj was looking for. It followed every item that happened to be drawn out of its dimension. He glanced back at his own trail. Incompatibility of matter or something, he mused.

This was the...let me see...four thousand eight hundred thirty ninth dimension he had tried in a period of over...um...forty-three hoojis (equivalent to twelve minutes and thirty-four seconds in Earth-dimension time, but since they in Trxymmm are much shorter lived than on Earth, it doesn't mean much either way).

So far kouj had found exactly nothing.

Or almost.

He had had a delightful stopover for a while in Rykuparr where that little bar-maid (she wasn't exactly a—all right, I'll stop saying it) had been overly friendly.

And now here he was on that backward planet of...what in the name of Goosi did they call it...ah, the book. Earth. What a guttural sound. Earth. Ughhh.

Nothing here either, he supposed, and yet...

The pen-atom detector clicked thoughtfully and then, as if summoning more courage, gave out a loud blast and pointed toward the far quadrant.

kouj (you always, always spell it with a small k, it being a proper name) immediately lit out for the spot.

It was a huge building with words upon it:

GROCTER AND PAMBLE SOAP COMPANY
HOME OF SWISH : the MIRACLE DETERGENT FOR ALL YOUR
HOUSEWORKING CARES!! WISH WASH? SWISH WASH!!!

This cryptic message bore absolutely no meaning for kouj who passed through the porous red material and entered the building. And gasped...

And turned white...

And left that dimension with such an audible pop that several workmen in the soap factory looked to their boiling pots of SWISH.

kouj made his report briefly and to the point. Then he was stabbed and the evacuation of Trxymmm was begun.

Thousands and millions and billions boarded trans-temporal realigners and shoved off for parts and/or dimensions unknown.

To get away from that warped dimension within whose vicinity was Earth. To get away was their most earnest wish.

kouj's report?

What it said was that they were making a horrible chemical mixture that would rip space-time fabric for eons to come in that dimension. It seems they were even passing it off for some strange ritual utensil or something.

Since they were getting out anyhow, they didn't worry about the lost atomic. A little verraliumoid-metal cube like that if exploded, as it surely would be, since its controls were so easy a moron could operate them, would get them anywhere, no matter how far away they tried to get.

It seemed that the people of the dimensions were living on borrowed time. But that SWISH...

Mrs. Frenessi swore in three languages.

It was quite a verbal display and Mr. Frenessi was uncommonly proud of the woman he had wed.

"What's-a the matt, Viola," he enquired.

"Sa tam can-opener won't-a woik," she exploded, banging the little metal cube on the tabletop.

Mr. Frenessi chuckled softly, "How many-a years since you find-a that ting in-a you winda-box?" he asked.

"It's-a be close to seventeen years this-a month," she replied, "Why?"

"What-a you worry about it for all-a time? You haint-a got it to 'ork-a right-a yet..."

As a matter of fact, she hadn't. But perhaps some day.

Abnormality
June 1952

Although the night was warm, there was the inevitable chill that is found around graveyards, permeating the atmosphere of the old house.

The house stood on a hill on the outskirts of the Big Town and showed clearly that no one—human—had lived there for a great number of years. The doors sagged outwards as though they alone carried the weight of the world, and the windows were all the same; broken, with small, jagged frames of glass still in the panes.

Atop the four-storey house was a small dormer with a window that was distinctly different from the others. Although it was clouded with the blown dirt and dust of years, it remained unbroken.

Like a sentinel. Watching when the rest of the brood has fallen asleep.

Through the window, nothing could be seen, and yet there appeared to be a roiling, a swirling, which came from within. The effect was more than just unnerving. At least it was to Tommy Corkan who stood before the house, suitcase in hand, and stared up at the weather-beaten boards of the building that had, through the seasons, changed from a healthy white-washed shade to a dull, lifeless gray that resembled the skin covering a week-old cadaver. He shivered.

With a shrug to the so-called Gods of Chance, he hoisted his brown suitcase and trod the weed-overgrown path to the door. He had no trouble entering. The door creaked once with the tug he made on it, and fell with a crash and many puffs of dust onto the porch.

With another shrug he went inside.

There was a good reason for his being here, he mused, upstairs in the room he had chosen for sleeping. It was his malady. No, it would be more fitting to call it an abnormality. Yes, that was it. And not an abnormality that could be taken care of by ordinary medications. Or even the help of doctors. It was a defect with which he would have to cope himself. No one would be of any help. He took his jacket off in the dim, flickering glow cast by the aged oil lamp he had found. It was lucky that he had brought along some lighter fluid or the lamp would still be unlit and he would be in darkness. A frightening thought.

He had his shirt off and was sitting on the bed, made up with his own linens, smoking a cigarette, when he heard the noise.

Stiffening, he knew immediately where it had come from. The small dormer atop the house which had drawn his attention when he first arrived at the house. Probably a rat...he hoped.

With a small shiver he doffed the rest of his clothes.

...the sound came again.

This time it was easy to distinguish the sounds that were transmitted through the near-rotting ceiling to his ears. It was a rustling at first. As though something were coming awake after a long, deep sleep. Then there was a thud. The same kind of thud that might be made if a—for instance—bat...were dropping off a rafter where it had been sleeping. The next thing the listening man heard was a dragging or rustling. Like a long cloak or a pair of wings being brushed along the wooden boards as someone...or something...shuffled across the floor. Then it ceased.

Tommy Corkan sat on the edge of the bed, his head cocked to one side, listening. There was no further sound from above. He swung his legs up onto the bed and slid beneath the sheets.

He blew out the lamp and lay in the darkness that had suddenly become stuffily oppressive. His cigarette, that lay on the table, burning the half-corroded wood, glowed dully, casting hardly any light.

"It was a foolish idea, anyhow," he thought to himself, "Why come all the way out here from the Big Town. From the warmth and security of a penthouse apartment."

But he knew the answer even before he asked himself the question. It was his malady; no, he had decided he would call it an abnormality. He just couldn't stay in town another night. If anything should...but why worry? He was safe here. And in a few days the serum would have taken effect and he would be on the road to recovery.

Tommy clasped his hands behind his head and thought how, after the attack the night before, he had hurriedly gathered together a few clothes and then gone to his real estate agent. He had found the ideal escape refuge. This house. Immediately he had rushed out here. And everything was all right now.

Except...

The noise came again. This time it was nearer. Outside his window. A fluttering of wings or the rustling of a cape, he couldn't tell which. Instantly he was tensed. Tensed against whatever was outside that window.

The darkness outside the broken window was superceded by a bulky object. It was either lighter or darker than the night, for though details of it could not be made out, the shape was clear. It was a man.

With more of the rustling, the man dropped into the room. Tommy lay quite still for a moment, then with a swift motion, lit the lamp with his cigarette lighter.

The man who stood before him was tall and thin; almost to the point of being gaunt. His skin closely resembled the color of the house. A cadaverous gray. He was draped from head to toe in a red velvet cape that rustled as he walked.

"So it was a cape," mumbled Corkan as he gazed in fascination at the tall figure.

Atop his head the visitor wore a large opera hat that seemed to belong there. But the most striking thing about him, as was to be expected in a person of this sort, were his eyes.

They were deep-set beneath very thin brows and in their black depths lurked the terror of age-old myths that had suddenly materialized. They smoldered and burned with an unearthly light that hypnotized and dulled the senses.

With a mental lurch, Tom Corkan pulled his gaze away from the man's eyes and stared at the rest of his visitor's face. It was deathly white around the mouth with a delicate nose, high cheekbones, and a red slash of a mouth from which protruded two obviously razor-sharp incisors that were a dull yellow in color.

"You're a vampire, aren't you," said Corkan, realizing how foolish the question was even as he said it. He hoped for a negative answer, but knew that it would not be.

"Yes," was the reply in a sibilant whisper.

"I had hoped I could escape. A little more time and I could have gotten over my abnormality. Why did you have to waken tonight?" And Tommy Corkan shrugged, threw off the covers, and with a hunching of his shoulders advanced upon the visitor; half-man, half-bat.

The tall, thin vampire looked startled for a moment and then instinctively shrunk back. He screamed once and then Corkan was upon him. The attacker sunk his perfectly normal teeth into the throat of the vampire.

Through a haze of red, Corkan mumbled, "You should never have come here tonight. You see, I have a very unusual abnormality. I have to drink the blood of vampires."

The vampire couldn't hear him.

The Ultimate Fanzine
October 1952

It came to me one night as I was listening to a tv show with the title, *What's Your Hobby, Bobby?*

Since my name is not Bobby, I decided that it didn't particularly matter what my hobby was. But then I gave it another thought and realized with something of a start that there was a cavity in my, till then, full life.

What was my hobby?

Girls? Making money? Girls? Enjoying life? Girls? Hell, No!

I read science fiction from way back and knew that the time had come. The day of the "true awakening" was at hand. (Oh my aching back.) All sfen must have one hobby. Publishing a fanzine.

So I grudgingly gave in to the little purple fanzine bug with the blood of pure mimeo ink and set about making plans to publish my FANZINE TO TOP ALL FANZINES.

First of all, it was to be a pocket-sized (that's all the rage now you know), 200-page, deckle-edged on gold plate with stained silver head and tail bands on top. It would feature as its cover an original Finlay illustrating the lead novelette which would be the latest in the Gods series by A. E. van Vogt entitled GODS OF THE GODS. The back cover would be a rare and famous painting from the Louvre, painted in 4,330,000BC by a little known artist named Ug-Mlook. It was called View of Demented Subway Chasing Errant Gum Machine. Inside artwork was to be by Finlay, Lawrence, Norman Rockwell, Cartier, Rod Ruth, Emsh, Orban, Rogers, Poulton, da Vinci, Terry, Michelangelo, Rockwell Kent, and for incidental decorations or things like that, Hannes Bok would do something or other.

The story lineup for the first issue would not be pretentious, but would show the readers that we held a great deal of promise. What was planned were some stories called:

"The Last City" (latest of the "City" series) by Clifford Simak

"Rhysling Meets the Wolf Man" by Robert A. Heinlein

"Androids Eternal" by Isaac Asimov

"I Was Trapped in a Lemurian Brothel" by Richard S. Shaver

THE GREY LENSMAN STRIKES BACK (part 1 of 312 chapters) by E. E. Smith

"Green Fury" by Eric Frank Russell

"Abraham Schwartz on Vishnu" by L. Sprague de Camp

"Dracula Returns" by Bram Stoker

"Journey to the Center of Nowhere in 30 Days" by Jules Verne and selected short stories.

The articles would be of interest to both avid fan "in-the-know" and casual readers. Among which would be:

"Science Fiction and Great Britain" by Winston Churchill

"How I Review Books Without Opening Them, or, Telepathy In Your Spare Time" by Bob Tucker

"The South Views Science, Fiction, and Revolt" by Lee Hoffman

"How I'm Going to Kill Beale" by Max Keesler

"How I'm Going to Kill Keesler" by Ken Beale

"How I'm Going to Kill All Earth" by Adolf Hitler (in collaboration with C. Williamson Degler)

and space filler science shorts by John W. Campbell, Jr., Bill Venable, and Willy Ley.

Now that the content was set, I had to think up a name for the fanzine. Something snappy like *Science Fantasy Bulletin*, or *Oopsla!* Or *Pendulum* or *Quandry* or something. Hmmmmmm, what to call it. Then I had it! I would call it Belcherone, in memory of the old Greek god, then I almost went into hysterics when I realized what I could abbreviate it to. Oh, happy day!

I was all set. I could start immediately.

"...so until tomorrow on WXEL, we return to test pattern and tone."

I turned off the set and went to bed.

The Logical Insanity
November 1952

We were not only taken by surprise, but their appearance left us in a state of amazed shock, so much so, that the Narl had landed their ships in Moscow and New York, in Paris and the Vatican, in Ankara and Munich, in fact everywhere, before we knew what was happening.

Their ships dropped out of the skies on a clear, wintry day in February. They skimmed down like a smooth, round rock on water and bumped almost imperceptibly onto the white-covered turf before the White House. I was there with the President, playing a little golf. He had been inaugurated a few weeks before and needed liaison men as much as he needed a vote of confidence. The ships opened and they emerged one at a time, seemingly unaware of the fact that we had drawn our guns (you see there was a segment of the National Guard on hand—I don't remember why just now) and they were leveling them at them as they stepped out of the cigar-shaped vehicles. They stood about three feet tall and looked humanoid to all but the very closest scrutinization. Their skin was a very faint bluish tinged epidermis with the coloring just barely showing superimposed, it seemed, over their lustrous white. Their six-fingered hands were webbed and they carried themselves with arrogant buoyancy that left no doubt as to the esteem they held themselves in.

Seven of them came toward the President, the Guardsmen, and myself. They walked casually, almost too casually, and then suddenly stopped, slung a metal box with a multi-faceted crystal in a socket on the face of a small dolly and pointed it in our direction. Contrary to what we had expected, having heard stories and seen motion pictures of like events, not one of the Guardsmen fired nervously at the aliens. They all stood as we, rooted to the spots in which they had stopped.

"...frxsbbl margraff klinect mencinne-okatto naowhere as friends to live beside you as brothers and contribute to your progress," the mechanically nasal voice emerged from gibberish into understandable English. "We are here from (the concept wasn't too clear at this point though we gathered that it was from an immeasurable distance away). Our voyage has been a long and tiresome one and we ask for no more than routine cordiality, in exchange for which we will bestow our advanced scientific knowledge upon you."

The President leaned forward, subtly empowered to speak for us all and hoping that the voice-box could decipher what he was saying, "Why have you come here? Why do you want to do this for us?"

"We must live with you in the Galactic culture, must we not?" twanged the voice-box. "Thus we must educate you. We come not as conquerors, but as fellow thinking beings." We shivered a little at this, imagining what any other "thinking" beings in the universe might look like, for these aliens seemed to have a quality about them that frightened us.

However, nothing more untoward than what we had seen, seemed to be about them, so they were led, as all delegations, to the reception room where The President, myself, and nine or ten other top men in the government, and a horde of Guardsmen listened to them. They told us about the trackless wastes of space and of the armada of teaching-ships (as they called them) which had ventured from their home star. They informed us of the 98 other ships, exactly like the two on the White House lawn, which rested in other parts of the world, carrying out the same task these representatives were.

In exchange for an opportunity to excavate for fuel for the return trip and provisions, they would not only give us the greatest gift ever dreamed about in the mind of Man. One hundred percent logic. They would subtly alter the brain patterns of every living man, woman, and child in the world to make them think accurately, emphatically, and lucidly. Their gift of unhampered logic would be the greatest step forward for man since he had emerged from his primeval cave-depths.

The President was all for it. He got in touch with the heads of the other great nations in the world and found to his surprise that they too had been offered the gift and were chomping on the reigns to receive it. A meeting was called of all the government heads in the U. N. headquarters in New York, and the date was set for a week later.

Came the day of the meeting and such co-ordination and accordance of thought would have done the peace-lovers of the world good to have seen. The decision was reached within a matter of an hour and the aliens left for their ships, to plunge upward into the stratosphere to loose the network of rays that would stabilize mankind and give him one hundred percent logic.

Invaders come in many guises, and the saying about Greeks bearing gifts is not an empty one. Why should a race three feet tall worry themselves about ray guns and killing and fighting and losing their own people, when to defeat another race all they had to do was use subterfuge?

Yes, they gave us logic, unimpaired logic, thorough logic. But it was our downfall, not our awakening. For within twenty minutes after their network of rays had started, employing the one thing we could have used against that awful weapon—our agreement and trust—every single human being in the world was hopelessly insane.

Did you ever think what *complete* logic could do to a person? Prevent him from seeing the beauty of a sunset...break it down into: one G-type sun, disappearing behind a range of sedimentary mountains due to the revolving of the earth on its axis. It would prevent him from seeing beauty, from seeing the subtle nuances of everyday life. It would furnish, instead, for him, a bare, sterile and coldly logical existence. Madness.

What S-F Means to Me
November 1952

What science fiction means to me. Hmmmm. That's an interesting question, you know. I've often wondered myself just why I spend my money on hordes of pulps that shed on my floors and which I may never get to read. I've often wondered why I put every other cent I own into a fanzine that inevitably will milk me of every cent I possess or have hopes of possessing.

I guess, now that I put a little more thought to the problem, that s-f DOES mean a great deal to me else I wouldn't waste my time with it.

Since the requirements for this contest are that I be dead serious (serious, that is) and not goof off, I guess I'll have to discard the whole ginger-peachy idea I had for telling you that I was a constipated engram in human form and really analyze my plight.

Damn you, Brown!

At any rate, the whole thing seems to simmer down to this. I've always been a pretty frustrated little kid, seeing as how I was just about the only Jewish fellow in the town of my age and had to fight for my blighted life darn near every day because it seems the other kids in town realized Jews aren't as good as human beings. Add to that the fact that I was always peanut-sized and you could whiff me away with a good breeze from your GE, and you can see that I was piling up inhibitions and complexes by the carton-full. Thus, when I came upon science fiction (lying in a gutter clutching a Bergey TWS to its chest) I found a literature wherein the ideas I had long upheld, held sway.

It spoke in grandiose terms of the equality of men, of the casual intermingling of races, of the racing adventure of just living in a world where science prevailed. It opened unto me the portals of worlds I had long dreamed about. Though IVANHOE, LES MISERABLES, JANE EYRE, and *Walt Disney's Comics and Stories* had been consumed in great quantities by myself through the years, this was the ultimate thrill for me. It embodied all I'd ever seeked after. It suited me to the proverbial T.

Then came fandom.

And I found a group of people whose only cohesive force was a general liking for S-F and a concerted liking for other people who were individual albeit off-their-rockers. And I felt a kinship immediately with these crazy, wonderful people who wrote in to magazines and burbled at great length on topics which were obviously influenced by the fans' thinking. I joined the Cleveland Science Fiction Society. I went to the Midwestcon. I started publishing a fanzine. I went to the Chicon. I suddenly found to my delight (and most of the time fright) that I had been heard of before.

What's that? I've gotten off the subject? I don't think so. Because you see, when you write an article of this sort, you speak from the heart. None of this mock humor of false modesty which curdles you when you read it. I speak the truth for those who wish to listen.

That it makes dull reading...I suppose. That Norm will junk it...I suspect. That I don't give a damn...I'm sure.

But in any event, I'm glad to dickens I unburdened myself. This, I guess, has been sticking in my craw and had to be said in one way or t'other. Any way you look at it, "It is a proud and lonely thing to be a fan."

Plague Planet
December 1952

I'm the last one. There are no more Martians here. We weren't always "Martians," this wasn't always "Mars." We had another name then. We lived on another world, it seems. Things are so different, so unreal, now. It was all so wonderful before...before *they* came. It was a world of rolling pink hills and fertile valleys. It had thin, ivory-walled cities that rose from the sides of the canals like white wraiths in the afternoon mists. It had laughing pink people, their so well regulated lives spent in calm endeavor, looking forward to the years ahead. We did not have space travel. We had no need for it. A happy and contented people feel no need for sojourning into realms too limitless to realize their potential.

We lived happily, dreamily if you will, in a world of complete joy that was from complete understanding of each other, we lived thus until...

It was in the four thousandth year of our Enlightenment. It was the beginning of a new decade, a new and more full era. We were in the midst of celebrating, the long streamers falling through the softly lighted byways of our cities, the people dancing and laughing, their luminous, red eyes glowing with reflected happiness. Then we heard it off somewhere above us. A throb. A deep, sonorous sound that somehow chilled us. For we knew that it was a spaceship even before it landed; there has been a good deal of talk about that but none of us "Martians" ever told them that we knew they had made it across the age old gulf of space to us.

It blossomed forth like some monstrous flower, a red glare in the night. Amid the blast of sound and light we saw a splinter of metal come hurtling down toward us. As the sound waves passed up and down a nerve-wracking sonic scale a note of what was to come was struck. For the more frail towers of our city began to tremble and shake and suddenly with a crash they fell into the streets, streets where debris had not lain for three thousand years. And then the rocket landed. It... it...was the first peal of doom, that landing.

They came out of the ship. As we have two arms, they had two arms. As we have two legs, they had two legs. As we were possessors of two eyes and a brain and an upright torso and opposed thumbs, so they too had these things. But they were subtly different. Five of them there were. They walked upright and greeted us in a phonetic tongue a linguist among us deciphered and translated in minutes.

"We have come as your friends." That is what their first words were to us. "We have come as your friends." And the frighteningly funny thing about it was that they *were* our friends. They had been conditioned thoroughly; there would be no fighting, no war, no conquered people, no conquerors. They were our friends. But even if they were unaware of it, they harbored death for us all.

We took them into our homes. We made of them brothers and son and husband. For three months we went on thus. And then the "diseases" began. Limbs were contorted, eyes bulged out, faces assumed horrible expressions. And then the deaths. Left and right they dropped like flies. We never knew what happened.

Finally, one of our most learned scientists gathered that the Earthmen had brought with them different germs, unnatural to "Mars" that, in their alien-ness, brought about horrible sickness and most painful death.

After weeks, the plant life began to suffer. Our crops began to wither in their fields, the productivity of our planet began to fail. We were in desperation. And still the deaths.

Then it ceased.

Yes, I'm the last "Martian" on "Mars." But not for the reasons you might think. You see, all the "Earthmen" died shortly, and in desperation, to preserve our race, for our planet was dying...

They all went to Earth.

All but me. I'm the last Martian...on Mars, that is.

Not THAT Again!
a short article voicing a gripe
29 December 1952

Remember this: "The mutants lurked silently behind the buildings, for they feared the wrath of an aroused humanity. With their telepath faculties (known as the Skrownge faculty) they plucked fresh mangoes from the cart of Tony the fruit peddler and prepared, re-nourished, to do battle with *Homo Sapiens*—on his way out."

Or: "Bat Birdbath came screaming down into the attitude of Bulbofagg, a tiny planetoid seven billion light bulbs from Saul. He cut out his heart...er...his super-hyper-drive for the landing...and at that point a tall, lame, spaceman stepped out of the tail assembly while in hyperspace and was crushed to a pulp, proton orange-squeezer in a tan hand; his other hand was orange with red dots."

And yet even: "'How will your time machine work,' said lovely Drusilla Dreck to Professor Frnf, 'I want to go with you into the old times of our gu-lorious pu-lanet!' The Professor told her how the id particles of the supra-menslatory-interdirectional-hypersensitivity no nothing-rehabilistrator combined with the glop to make one force field that would send them into the carboniferous era to bring back samples, he reminded her, of the head of a man who would not be born for a week and three days. 'Oh,' said Drusilla."

There are a few samples of what irk the devil out of me. This is reputed to be the "Age of Science Fictional Maturity" or some such no-goodnick name. I seriously doubt the seriousness with which the reporters of such phrases are imbued. It seems too naïve to believe that in this day and age of the moth-eaten alien invasion and the hunted et being tracked through hamlet and ophelia (er...pardon me) and town, and the noxious recurrence of transplanted a) detectives, b)westerns, c) old love stories, and d) baseball yarns to some unbelievable culture or orb a million years and/or miles from Podunk, that *this* could be *that* era.

I am just a little sick to my belly of the aliens who are going, by secret and ultra-scientific hook or crook to do something to Earth, Sol, and/or (again) its inhabitants, but who, by their ultra-scientific ignorance, let one (mind you, one) Earthman know about their plans and he, equipped with nothing more than a roll of scotch tape and two reading copies of the latest Spillane monstrosity, foils them by either warping space and transplanting the entire alien galaxy or by knocking off the one alien agent who has not told the "old folks at home" where he was going, so Earth is saved.

I am sick to death of Our Hero going into the death-infested prison planet to get one man...and comes out as nood as goo with but one or two scratches on his left thigh. I am revolted at androids who are suddenly aware that they aren't humans. I regurgitate at tales which end, "...for you see (Ta-ra-ta-ta-ta!), I'm blind!" I am thoroughly disgustipated at a yarn which propounds the theory that time is the 4 dimensional extension of Earth. All these and the ones about robots, taking over the world, and a member of any proposed culture who, to discover the bad side of that culture is first ostracized. Oh, do the old hackneyed plots give me mental diarrhea!

I have read, in the past three months, seven, get that, seven s-f yarns that ended up with the hero being eaten by either a planet or by the aliens—for one reason or another. If I had *my* way, the authors would be the ones eaten!

I'm no genius like Bester or Jones, to put out stories like DEMOLISHED MAN or THE TOYMAKER. I'm no clever-headed scribe like Guinn with his BEYOND BEDLAM. But I *am* a reader who is sick to death of the story like Heinlein's PUPPET MASTERS (old hat alien invasion) which is saved and made terrific by the writing. Ghod prevent the field from a period of stagnation like unto the Gernsback crud era. If anything is to save s-f from remaining "pulp fiction," it must be a rebirth of the Campbell days when John W. was first scrapping the SCIENCE fiction for the science FICTION.

So help me, if I read one more story about the fact that I'm property, I will go slowly batty and send a package with *me* inside to the author of same. Warning authors, if you don't want Ellison as a paper weight, to drive you slowly out of all your minds...get some new ideas and start writing them. Then sell 'em!

THE END (thank goodness!)

General Consensus
1953

All right, it's been bandied back and forth enough, what's the answer? Is fandom improving or degenerating?

My answer to the problem: To quote from one of those obnoxious but oft times searching blurbs the hucksters use on their motion pictures, "There ain't much, but what there is is cherce."

The last ten years have seen a metamorphosis striking in its enormity, which has taken fandom and turned it guts side out. Fandom. In the 1920s (late) and 1930s (early) it was a group of persons who gathered together to talk science-fiction, fantasy, and/or science. Fandom now? A bunch of people, ranging from the younger set, typified by the youth who reads all the promags to the BBBBBNF, who casually throws at you, "I don't *bother* to read StF." Fandom is now a fairly well-knit organization resembling the United States in more than one respect. It is a group of rugged individualists (well, individualists anyhow) who say what they want and do what they want just the way they want and damn the slings and arrows of outrageous Watkins.

What holds them together is the umpteenth wonder of the modern world if we consider King Kong in there somewhere. Some say the love of SF, though you and I both know that's a hunka hokum. My boy Veriabobble seems to think it's egoboo. I know several others that hold it's the free-and-easiness of fandom that allows a man to say and think what he wants, delve into old mysteries and traverse new channels, more than any other group. I choose not to comment upon that, myself.

But I do want to make several pointed queries as to whether fandom is climbing that ladder or slipping into the quagmire.

First of all let's try to rid ourselves of thinking of fandom as one separate unit that has passed through stages. Fandom is roughly divided in half. The pre-40 era when SF and science-hobbying held 'em together, and the post-40 age when they went off at God-knows-what-all tangents in the pursuance of their fanish ways.

Somehow or other fandom has bred the New Fan; a man of odd tastes, of odd thoughts, a man who reads very little, if any, StF, who publishes numerous fanzines, corresponds heavily, is well-liked, and is considered all around a gen-oo-wine 14 carat Big Name Fellow.

All right, let's admit Maxie Keasler typifies the New Fan. He's not alone. There are dozens of others. What are they doing to this institution known as fandom?

How can we say they are making it better or worse? We can't tell— seeing as how we have never gone through this stage. But suffice it to say that the Max Keasler of today would have *absolutely* no place in the fandom of pre-40. He would have been an oddity, something to be looked at and say, "Doesn't *read* SF? Then why is he a fan?"

Quite obviously, the answer is this: He isn't a fan.

Drop that Boa Constrictor, Max, till I elucidate upon the theme. Now I'm not saying my boy isn't a fan. This may sound like sheer contradiction at first when you read the sentence preceding this paragraph, but here's what I mean, and I hope you and Max will forgive me for using him as the guinea pig, but he is an outstanding example of what I mean.

Max is that new species of fan that has been in the works for a decade or so. He is a mutant breed that is now coming into prominence. Five years ago he couldn't have been BNF. Ten years ago he certainly would not have been at home in fandom. Only now, as with humanity itself, we are prepared for him.

In other words...Fandom is splitting. Now the theme of SF for the sake of SF is not the thing that will hold fen together. It will be the auras of their own personalities interlocking to provide companionship over great distance which will make them want to be called "fan."

Just as in the late 30s the science-hobbyist paled into insignificance, so the purist who is in fandom *only* for the reading (and conversing) of

StF will go off to himself and be a *science-fiction fan* and the Keaslers et al. will go off and be just...*fans*.

But whether this is good or not is something which will have to be witnessed to be analyzed. I'll be blamed of I'll commit myself on this point. But I will say this: There are some eye-openers on the way.

There's no holding back tomorrow...as who wants to.

Birdbath to Bulbofagg
1953

from *Vega #7*

SALUDE: I find myself transplanted, so to speak. From the pages of the short-lived *Foo-View* magazine of Barclay Johnson, which, I'm sad to say, has gone to its eternal resting place in that Great Wild Hair Session up yonder. This column has no set purpose, insofar as I can tell, save to occasionally provide a chuckle or two and/or provide a bit of information hitherto unknown. If I succeed every once and again in this most difficult of pursuits, I will consider the time and effort spent on this column most rewarding. The foregoing constitutes a welcoming address. Take it for what it's worth. Which isn't much, of course.

DEPARTMENT OF ASININE ANACHRONISMS: Ever notice that a *book* with ragged edges is called "deckle-edged" and costs more because of it, but a *magazine* with ragged edges is a "cheap pulp" and is a disreputable, if you'll pardon the term, publication. Oh, well, only the publishers can figger *that* one out, I can't.

DAMN THOSE COPYSMITHS! Did you ever *really* listen to some of those soap ads that are circulating (and poisoning) through the atmosphere? I mean for instance the one for a well-known soap which says, "Nature's chlorophyll is in every cake of — —, that's what makes — green. Though no medical value is placed upon the chlorophyll in —, you should know that —'s same formula is..." In other words, they are saying, "Well, you stupid characters won't even buy earplugs nowadays, unless they've got chlorophyll in 'em, so we'll put some of the crap in our soap. Now understand that the chlorophyll won't do a damned thing, but if it makes you happy, it's in there." Oh brother, does that make me so sick I could vomit! How stupid can the populace get?

MUTATION: By now you've seen the new AVON SF AND FANTASY READER. I am truly shocked. When I saw Don Wollheim last year (at the time he was the head bigwig in the stfantasy line), he told me that the reason for the poor quality of the AVON FANTASY READER was that the company demanded he use a cover layout with a near-naked femme on it. I believed him since there was no reason not to, but now with Sol Cohen in as editor, the new mag is really high-class, featuring good material, fine authors, and beautiful illos. One of two things: either Wollheim was the one responsible for the atrociousness of the old Avon pubs, or Sol Cohen has swung the Big Boss's mind to the fan's view. Either way, it's a turn to the better, for the new mag is some 300% better than the old jobs.

...AND WHY SHOULDN'T I?: Everybody seems to be predicting like mad nowadays, so why shouldn't Ellison jump into the fray with both webbed feet and say that the second-best mag in the stfantasy field today is Lester del Rey's tremendous new *Fantasy Magazine* which is like a breath of old *Unknown*. Being an *Unk*-lover from 'way back and having a fairly well filled-out collection of *Unk*s, I know an *Unknown*-type story when I see one (i. e., mature fantasy with a tinge of adult humor), and take my word for it, keeds, *FM* has about five of them. "The Night Shift" by Frankie Robinson is a small masterpiece (and has been already accepted for a new anthology from World Publishing. I'm bashfully happy to say that li'l ole noodle-head Ellison brought the yarn to the attention of the anthologist. Awright, awright, so I *am* tooting my own horn, so watt?) and Poul Anderson's immensely entertaining "Ashtaru the Terrible" are both sweet gems. Oh, man, this mag is the answer to a deprived *Unk*-reader's dreams.

OH, YEAH: Read *Science-Fiction Plus*? If not, don't. If did, my sorrow goes out to you. You have suffered greatly. 1933, here we come!

ALL QUIET ON THE FMZ FRONT: I haven't had a good argument in the last few weeks so why not start a lulu while I'm at it? All righty, let's. To wit: Redd Boggs is a crumbum who likes to pick people apart because of his own psychological maladjustments. Bill Venable is a square. Donald Susan is (oh, oh, Donald Susan is 300 lbs....) a great guy. Jonny Magnus uses real blood to reproduce two-color illos in *SF*. Joel Nydahl eats moths. I'm waiting.

LINGUISTICS AND SUCH: In an ever-increasing awareness on the part of your reviewer to indulge in highly elevated experiments, I present a paragragh of commentary broken down into basic sound-English as prescribed by G. B. Shaw and Dolton Edwards:

Ser iz a colum uv fanzeen revewz sat haz alredy started en Zienz Fikshun Kwarterlee bi Calvin Tomuz Bek. Hee zeemz too bee zinzeer en hiz reevuws, tow hee cood doo mor than hee haz zo far. Calvin zeemz too bee tring too doo ay good job, zo whi dunt tu fanz la uf him alreddy?

Weeeeeeeew! And if you think it's easier writing that than reading it, just try it, go ahead.

QUESTION OF THE WEEK: Saw a letter from the rottenest character in fandom in the latest *Planet Stories*. Question: Is that negro-baiter of a crumbum Sigler coming back into fandom? Cops!

STORIES THAT SHOULD BE PUT INTO BOOK FORM: POLICE YOUR PLANET in *SF Adventures* by Erik van Lhinn ... NULL-ABC in *aSF* by McGuire and Piper ... THREE IN ONE by Damon Knight in *Galaxy*. Of course, they'd all have to be expanded... Heh, heh, I may be stupid, but I ain't dumb!

RHETORIC: Who is prettier in fandom than Mari Wolf or Bea Mahaffey or Judy May or Miss X. (A great many of you know who I mean, but I'll be stuffed with prunes afore I'll say it)?

ANYONE WANT A DARTBOARD?: I have a few pictures of me left that I'll be glad to mail to you upon receipt of a check for fifteen million dollars and the top of your mother's head. I can't keep the damned things around here, they're drawing flies like mad. Ho weel...

POOPED: Which indicates I'm through for thish. Hasta Banannas!

This column has been fortified with chlorophyll!

from *Vega* #8

The tallys came in; both to Joel and myself, for a great many of you read both *Vega* and *Science Fantasy Bulletin*, and it was evident, to even the most blind, that BtoB flopped quite badly. Whether it was the seeming disunity of format, whether it was the fact that (as one person put it), "I talked a lot and said very little," or for some reason unlisted but too obvious to be recognized, BtoB came off rather badly. Unlike many fan writers, I dislike writing poor material.

Since I have no foolproof criterion for writing a good column, I think perhaps it would be best if I patterned them after my own column in *SFB*, *Burblings*, which seems to get good ratings no matter how loosely it is written. Or on the other hand, perhaps one that mimics my editorials would be better—i. e., taking just one topic and expanding on it in an informal discussion manner to get a sort of an article, junior grade. I'm not certain which would meet with more universal approval. I have a number of good ideas for article/ columns. Such as "Up Popped Sheckley" which could discuss the merits of the biggest writing sensation in s-f history since Weinbaum, or "Why Do They Underrate Morrison?" which might offer a defense of an extremely good stf writer who has been sold down the river so to speak, or "The Spate Continues" in which I might analyze the new stf mags and try to fathom which ones will last, etc.

I don't know how these sound to you, so I'm just going to go ahead with an informally insulting column this issue, and let either Joel or myself know which sounds best to you, and next issue will see the introduction of said style.

CONFUSION PAR EXCELLENCE...Jimmy Taurasi, who leaps up and down with clapping hands and clucking tongue every time a new prozine flops onto the already sagging market, seems to have confused everyone in fandom with his clever and sly hints dropped in the bi-weekly (supposedly) *Fantasy Times* to the effect that there is a *Universe Science Fiction* being published by Century Publications. But when I look at the publishing credits in my copy of *USF*, I see it is pubbed by George Bell of Bell Publishing. I don't think they're confusing it with *Fantastic Universe* (the monster 50¢ job), but are talking about two different mags. If so, then we've completely missed the Century *Universe* in this neck of the woods and I implore someone out there to either shut Taurasi and mad babblings up, or send me a copy of the blarsted thing!

Eh keed, how you like BtoB now? Is better yet? Non? Yes? Mebbe? FLASH!...Joel Nydahl does NOT eat moths...salamanders...!

Oh hell, what can I talk about? Did you ever get the feeling that you wanted to pitch onto your head with fatigue? But then you have some crumb of an editor like Nydahl on your back screaming frantically that "I need your colyum kwik, you clod!" So I have to tear myself away from my thirty-five beautiful concubines and write this monstrous piece of sludge so you chowderheads can nod sagely and write in something like, "Why don't you tell that Ellison creep to lie down? His column is beyond a doubt one of the dumbest things I ever read! I din't unnerstan' it..." And the note, scrawled on a piece of butcher-shop Kraft paper in red crayon, will be signed: Max Lump.

There's gotta be an easier way to get egoboo.

ENTRANCE EXTRAORDINAIRE...Since I first started drawing my copyrighted BEM, I have been searching around for another little cartoon figure that I could slap into situation strips strictly for laughs. And I think I've come up with one at last. His name is

MAX J. RUNNERBEAN

and he looks something like this—

I intend to start using Max J. in *SFB* soon, but I thought I might just introduce him around first and give you all a look at him. I've been told that he resembles in some respects Max Keasler's malicious-looking little Bullet-head, but I should like to stress most emphatically that he is nothing at all like that odd character Maxie was prone to whomp up for a number of years. Max is, though he looks formidable, one of those poor milquetoasty characters that winds up with flowerpots on his head, tire treads on his stomach where busses mistakenly re-routed, and a general all-around poor disposition from too many people taking too many advantages of him.

I think the reason Max J. and his ilk are popular is the same reason Mr. Peepers and Charlie Chaplin gained fame. They portrayed the average man who is always getting the raw deal instead of the "everything ended all sweetness and light" character of modern fiction. I hope you like Max J. He hates you, y'know.

POOSH!...I'm tired as all get out (so why don't you?) so I'd best sign off right in here somewhere. Oh, there's a nice clean spot on the paper where, if I'm careful, I could type those clever six letters which spell out

THE END

from *Vega* #9

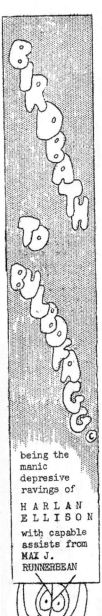

being the manic depresive ravings of

H A R L A N
E L L I S O N

with capable assists from

MAX J. RUNNERBEAN

AND IF YOU THINK I ENJOY HOLDING UP THIS CARD FOR THAT ELLISON CRUM, YOU ARE MOST SADLY MISTAKEN

WELL DOO DEE DOO DEE DOO...how ya like that? The B to B came in in third place. And behind Mez Bradley, and Uncle Robertuck too. Say, that is some sort of an honor, ain't it. I could bill myself as: HARLAN ELLISON: ALWAYS BEHIND TUCKER AND BRADLEY'S BEHIND or something. Speaking of Tuck's article in this issue of *Vega*, which we weren't, I might as well place a dandy li'l plug for a Tucker piece coming up in *Science Fantasy Bulletin* called "So Long, Joe" which will blow a portion of the fan ranks as wide open as Tallahassee on a Saturday night. It will be featured in the *SFB* Annual, overdue from February, but out very soon. Anyone who doesn't get *SFB* steady will have to pay 35¢ for this dee-lishus issue, but *SFB* subbers get it with their sub.

AND AS LONG AS WE'RE ON THE SUBJECT...the *SFB* annish, which may as well get plugs wherever it can, will be an innovation in annuals. We're not striving for bulk. *SFB* has that every issue. What we want is real quality! So far the lineup is thus:

1) A scratchboard cover by David English. The first time he has ever done any scratchboard work

2) "Ponce De Leon's Pants" by Mack Reynolds— the short story no prozine would buy because it was taboo. *SFB* publishes it with illos by English before it is used as the title story for Mack's first one-man, anthology

3) "The Conquest of Nearby Space" by Willy Ley—illos by Michael Frazier—the latest on space travel by Ley

4) "The Twilight World" by Paul Cox—illos by Rotsler

5) "Imposter" by Bill Venable—illos by Venable

6) "Mr. Disney and Tyrannosaurus Rex" by Richard Elsberry—illos by Lawrence Hekelman

7) "You Can't Beat Columbus!" by A. Charles Catania—illos by Robert Athearn.

8) "So Long, Joe" by Bob Tucker—illos by Bob Peatrowsky

9) "How to Be a Science Fiction Critic" by Robert Bloch—illos by Bill Venable

10) "The Second Most Important Man in the World" by Gregg Calkins—illos by Phyllis Hiller

11) "Report on Seventh Fandom" by Charles Wells—illos by Vaughn Burden

12) "A Bit of Assistance" by Harlan Ellison—illo by Lynn Hickman

plus some other material that has come in and I've forgotten about, and other stf stuff that will have come in by the time you read this. If you want a copy, it will be out around the middle of June, send 35¢ CASH ONLY to Harlan Ellison, 12701 Shaker Blvd., Apt. #616, Cleveland 20, Ohio before June 10th, as there won't be any extra printed up.

PORTRAIT cF The
MODERN FAN

STATEMENT OF PERSONAL LEANINGS...for perhaps the first time in the past five or six years, a columnist is going to come right out and make a series of definite opinions that will leave no doubt whatsoever as to what he thinks on a certain subject. That subject is just this: Who are the best writers in the fan field?

You know, there is a difference between an actually *good* writer and a hack character that can turn out ream upon ream of sludge for the fanzine editor who requests it simply because a "name" is attached.

I won't say that Bob Tucker is the best writer in the field. Far from it.

For my top choices of the best writers in the field, for 1953, I'd like to nominate Fred Chappell, Rich Elsberry, Redd Boggs, Bill Venable, Larry Saunders, and Bob Silverberg.

Now I'll tell you why.

To make a GOOD writer, the fan must have a) style, b) talent, c) something to say, d) intelligence enough to say it properly, and e) a gimmick. Elsberry and Silverberg and Boggs to a certain degree have that certain manner of presentation that makes their work highly analytical. Not one single piece of work from Silverberg's fluent pen can be called hack. That is simply because Robert is a semi-perfectionist. The obvious amount of research that goes into every bit of material he issues is so clearly evident, that you are reassured at the very outset that what he has to say will be concise, accurate, and up-to-date.

Elsberry, on the other hand, cannot be trusted in what he says. For Rich (though I love him like a brother) is the type of writer who has an amazing facility of taking the most staid, obvious sentence and twisting it to make something entirely opposed come out of it. His inherent grasp of the field of semantics, and his native intelligence for misconstruing purposely what others say, and his overall method of presenting these semantically arranged arguements in an analytical manner so that they appear to be carefully thought-out, is magnificent.

Boggs is perhaps the "cleanest" writer in the lot. When he has

something to say he attacks the subject coolly from the front, takes it point by point, works to the end of the topic and leaves it, and you, with a thorough background in just what he is talking about and he has persuaded you, by the simple ploy of complete frankness, and honesty, that the conclusions he has reached should be yours. He is a cool number and thus convinces you because of his sureness.

Venable is a genius; has extreme writing talent, and any more would be like guilding the proverbial water-flower.

Chappell and Saunders are the two most underrated. Fred is beyond a doubt one of the most competent authors in the game, could sell widely to the pros if he'd stop his fanning for a time, and should be more highly recognized throughout fandom.

Such Chappell as "The Song, the Tree," and dozens of others that bear the unmistakable mark of brilliance steadily take first place ratings in the fanzines in which they appear and yet Fred still plods along, unrecognized. What does he have to do? Write something of the length and stature of the DECAMERON of Boccaccio or something of the sort?

And Saunders, whose rapier-sharp wit brought off one of the best hoaxes of all fan-time, THE FAN YEARBOOK hoax, is just coming up in the ranks, but watch him, for his talent is unmistakable. He has a way with words.

More of these folks and less of such fans as...

...well, they're all my friends, but I've told them to their faces and I'm not ashamed to say it here, since they know that no ill-feeling is meant. Such fans as Don Cantin, Bert Hirschhorn, Dick Clarkson, and over two hundred others that make *damned good* editors, but lousy writers. I mentioned the above three because they are three of my best friends and I'm certain they won't take offense. And yet, they have Names, and the faneds take any and all crud they whip out, lowering their reputations left, right, and indifferent. These fans should work ploddingly on one piece of mss. till they have it down as best they can, and then send it out, allotting their mss. so that only the best stuff sees print.

When a good piece, like for instance Clarkson's "Who's Crazy?" in *SFB* comes to light, it's lost amid the quagmire of slop that has overflowed from that source previously.

So, instead of it being acclaimed, the only reaction it gets is, "Well, it was good enough, but look at all his *other* stuff!"

A little patience makes perfection, would be a good motto for the writers in fandom to accept. And if the editors in fandom were a little more discerning about the stuff they accepted, like Silverberg and Calkins and Venable and Nydahl are, perhaps we wouldn't be hearing so many people damning fan-fiction everywhere.

For I've seen plenty of good fan fiction, but isn't it strange that I've never seen it in the fanzines edited by the fans who turn out hack for other fanzines. Paradox? I think not.

WHEEEEW!...apologies are in order for that last blast. Apologies are in order for me plugging my own mag in the first paragraph. (You cut them, Nydahl and you're a dead man!) Apologies for...oh hell... I apologize for breathing today. See you all next issue. Keep eating salamanders.

from *Vega* #10

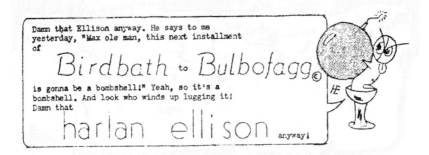

THE SEMENOVICH SLANDER CAPER...I dislike fighting. Ever since the sun-shiny Sunday afternoon when Harlan Ellison saw one of his best friends nearly ripped to shreds in a race riot in the quiet little town of Painesville, Ohio, he has never carried on a fight with a man or beast for very long. To fight is to indicate a marked deficiency of gray matter residing within the crevices of the head of the participants; and since I've always considered myself one to possess at least a modicum of intelligence, I have fought seldom and far between. My last fight was at the age of sixteen when a young man whom I later found out was an amateur boxer, referred to my religion in a most deprecatory fashion, and I took a good healthy swipe at his jaw. He thereupon swept up the floor with me, adding further impetus to my resolve never again to engage in pugilistic endeavors.

Howsoever, at this time I feel impelled to launch myself into a discussion which very probably may end in fist-swinging. I hope not—but, in the words of that great American philosopher, Joseph Semenovich, "That's how the ball bounces." You see, I realize that this column should not be written. It will only serve to strain relations that are already at the breaking point. I also realize that there is a certain element of immaturity in my doing this, but at the same time I am deriving pleasure out of it that is seldom equaled in a man's life. I had an acquaintance once who got no greater pleasure out of life than that which he derived from going into a random bar and starting a good rousing brawl. As I've said, I dislike fighting intensely but I pride myself on a tongue and a typer which can wield a suitable amount of cutting effluvium.

The whole trouble stemmed from the fact that I am also a damnably blunt individual. If I see a woman that has come to play canasta with my mother in my room, piddling around in my collection, I calmly tell

her to get the hell out of there lest I crown her one with an end table. Or if it displeases me to sit and listen to some inane musician who seems hell-bent upon "...splitting the ears of the groundlings...," I immediately stand up, swear a blue streak, and turn the Krauthead off. So it is that when I read a fanzine and am required, if I want the editor of that mag to send a letter of criticism to *my* zine, to write a letter commenting on same, I tell the truth and pull no punches. I have done this with numerous magazines, telling each editor exactly what I thought of his magazine, in a *constructive manner ONLY*. I have, at all times, taken a constructive approach to the problem, and in no way have I tried to be antagonistic. To my eternal regret, I foolishly supposed Joe Semenovich, editor of *Renaissance*, could take criticism that was intended in the best of faith. The letter appeared in the March 1953 issue of *Renaissance* and read in part:

> I am taken aback at the quality of crud you permit to grace what could be a most entertaining fanzine. I must start with Francis Bordna who, I hasten to state, does as creditable job of columning as I've seen in the last few months, but whose column is so be-riddled with errors that I feel I *must* comment in order of appearance...

Then I went on in as analytical a manner as I am capable of employing, and took Fran Bordna's column to task. It was a practice employed by everyone from Redd Boggs down to the lowliest neefan when talking about a magazine. I then said in the letter:

> It is reprehensible that you allow...Bordna to say anything she wants without verification. However, this is again, a column of opinion, and as such it is good. I just thought I'd bring facts up to date for you as it is interesting...

I later found out Bordna was a man, not a woman, but that was neither here nor there. You can see, from the very words printed in Joe's own magazine, that I was not out after blood, but trying to do him a service by commenting boldly on what I liked and disliked. I went on, later in the same letter, to remark:

MEMOIRS OF A FAN: useless piece of pre-convention slush that has very little point. It gives no useful or amusing info about the Baffalocon and if the reader didn't know it as such, he'd think what in the hell is going on around here, who cares who he got stewed with? At least from my angle that's what I thought ... SURE CONVERTS, etc.: not bad...at least readable. But not up to Toby's usual stuff, if you get what I mean ... AN ARTICLE FOR YOU: excellent piece of work. Enjoyably lucid ... STF IN HOLLYWOOD: could have been better, might make a novel feature if not handled in such a ponderous, heavy-handed manner...

And that is the important segment of this letter which started the ruckus off.

Now Joe, in the answer, right under my letter in that issue, was as nice as he could possibly be. He was pleasant, amiable, and seeming to take it on the chin. That was the outward appearance. Here's what went on underneath, that no one knew about. The thing that has culminated in Semenovich's frenzied attack on *SFBulletin* and his slanderous remarks in many fanzines, most lately *Vega*, last issue.

After I wrote the letter to *Renaissance*, I got a letter from Joe indicating that I was an idiot who could not see the innate beauty of a copy of *Renai*. Well, granted that I am an idiot, and granted that *I* can't see the beauty of *Renai*, let the other members of this fannish whirl speak of Joe's magazine (as a side-light, I chose *Vega*) and suggest that I not take any improbable crudzines such as —, —, —, and *Renaissance*. These are his words, not mine, and only to serve to indicate that Joe's mag could have stood improvement. Yet he went right ahead and got P. O.ed to an extreme and we began exchanging cutting letters. Granted I should have shut my head and stopped the thing before it got, as it is, out of hand. I did not. After he had covertly threatened to knock me out of fandom if I did not watch my step, I sent him a letter the first two paragraphs of which read:

Let's get one thing clear, brother, before this letter goes any further. If you're looking for a feud, a real live-action feud, I'm the boy to give it to you. I've never had one in fandom, but if, as a correspondent tells me, you're hashing up trouble in some of the other fmz letter columns for me, I'll lay into you with both barrels at the smoking stage and worry about the results while looking at your charred remains (fandom-wise speaking).

But if you try to keep it a polite interchange, then okay, but don't try any subversive shit brother, because I'm just waiting for a chance to bust you wide open. I don't like fighting, sword or pen, but you start any trouble and it won't be me that'll be out of fandom, that's for sure.

At this point, a good number of increasingly snide and insulting letters had been received from Joe, and I was getting word from fans in New York and thereabouts that he had been sending them letters for their correspondence columns in various fanzines, insulting me and calling me everything from a habitual narcotics imbiber to an escaped war prisoner from Dachau. *Of course* I got hot! Who wouldn't?

But back to the gory story. In the next letter Joe wrote these words to me:

In your letter to me you really bragged of constructive criticism—did you give me any? Really, did you? Damn, no, you didn't. You're just a little punk, a guy with an over-budding inferiority complex—and don't say you don't have one, "birdbath." ... You're a little hypocrite too, Phony. ... phony as they come. ... So you're going to kick me out of fandom, punk? Do you actually believe it means that much to me?—you have rocks in your watered brain! Try it, punk, try it. ... What irks me even more is that remark in the second paragraph, 'I don't like fighting, sword or pen, but you start any trouble and it won't be me that's out of fandom, that's for sure.' Now I don't mind most of that sentence, but when I read 'sword or pen' what am I to think? You little punk, just pick up a hand as if you're going to fight me physically, and I'll lay you on your ass. I can't stand little punks who say they're going to use their fists—I take great pleasure in throwing them out a *window*—through a window, yes, but not out a window; through a door, yes, but not out a window... ... And when this letter is completed, I will immediately write a letter to Karl Olsen (of *Komet*), asking him to forget about

the postcard I sent him to take out what I said about you.
Okay, punk, I started it—now it's your move. Am anxiously
awaiting your reply, punk.

Now I didn't know at the time whether to laugh myself into a
stroke, or sit there and ponder the obvious mental frailties of such a
warped and twisted mentality. The fellow obviously sounded like some
sort of a big-time gangster, with the thirteen or so "punks" he used in
one such letter.

However, by this time I had regained my composure and wrote
him an answer stating that if he wanted any further correspondence it
would be on a high level or not at all. He responded in kind, but a few
weeks after that I sent out *SFBulletin*. An issue which, to point up the
madness of the inevitable reply, was ranked as one of the best of the
year & which, among others, Mari Wolf referred to as "Powerful!" He
wrote me a letter which said, "Face it, Ellison, your zine isn't so hot..."
and much more of like nature. I was so infuriated by this that I ran the
letter, as much of it as I had space for and was of general interest (not
cutting it so it would seem I was in the right, as Joe later indicated) and
said under it that I would let the readers answer him. They did. With
thirty-five letters that compared Messr. Semenovich unfavorably with
(a) a Mongoloid Idiot, (b) a male donkey, (c) a ranting lunatic, and (d)
a jealous husband.

Joe, in the meantime, sent a letter of apology that he wanted run
in the *SFB* letter column. I DID NOT PRINT THE LETTERS OF THE
FOLKS WHO SAID HE WAS A CRUMB-BUM, but I *did* print his letter
of apology, referring, in the note under it, to the original argument as
"child's play," indicating that I should have been old enough not to get
into such a diatribe.

Since then, I have had sporadic and reasonably amiable relations
with Semenovich and even did an article for *Renaissance* (which he now
says, after holding it for five months, he cannot use; he hasn't bothered
to send it back, however). I thought all was settled and quiet, till this
letter popped up in *Vega* last month.

That is my side on it.

Got anything to say, Joe, me bhoy?

I'll be back next month, if I don't get a celluloid bomb in the mail
from a certain JS of Chicago, lately of Flushing-in-the-toilet, New York.
And BIRDBATH TO BULBOFAGG will tackle a more pleasant topic or

two, I trust. Perhaps an analysis of the differences between the old-time, dead-serious fanzines and the slush piles of today.

from *Vega* #12

APPRAISAL: I went back and looked over a few of the old-time fanzines that somehow or other I had managed to accrue. There were items like *Bizarre, Stardust, LeZombie,* and three or four others that were adjudged leaders in the field ten or so years ago. Then I came back to the present (rather more reluctantly than I wished) and took a look at the stack of fan magazines which had gathered on my desk during the last two weeks. There was a copy of *Vega* and a copy of *Destiny,* and there was a copy of the *Journal of Science Fiction* and a copy of my own *Science Fantasy Bulletin* (return—with addressee unknown)...all of which I put aside in a definite attitude of otherness, for they were not useful in the survey I was about to make.

You see, I was going to find out what had transpired in a decade to change the tenor of amateur publishing so radically. I gravely rubbed my jaw in contemplation of the survey at hand, for it was definitely one that needed to be made, and yet there was no logical way to do it. To assuage a reason for the change in attitude toward fanzine pubbing was to also point out the major (and in some instances, minor) trends in the fan world over a ten-year period. This was in no way a simple thing to do.

Perhaps, insofar as I can detect, the most influential two trends in fandom that affected the manner in which the modern fmz is edited were what I shall term the "Hate-all-Pros" trend and the "Lee Hoffman-laugh-minute" trend. The former crept insidiously into the thinking processes of most fen and slyly told them that the pros were filthy hucksters, to be sneered at upon any and all occasions, and exiled the pros from the fmz, where previously they had been the rule—not the exception. The latter was one that propounded the theory of, "I'm in it for the fun, and to hell with either prestige or hard work!" That Lee made a success of that theory is indication of the talent of the lass, and also a sad thing indeed. For it paved the way for multitudinous imitators whose paucive ilk are still stinking up the field.

Of a moment, let me insert something here: I may have neglected to tell you just what the attitude is. The attitude is one of sloppy, ill-framed, worthless, quality-minus magazines featuring material and art of a like nature. The day of the neat fanzine with the gorgeous illos by Bok, Gaughan, Arfstrom, etc. is long since flitted. We now get a magazine like *Whispering Space* with a front cover that appears at first glance to be the work of a Mongoloid Idiot three-year-old drawing on a sheet of corrugated cardboard with an eyebrow pencil held between her big and second toes on the left foot. And material of a caliber to evoke nothing so much as upchucking sounds and an overpowering urge to head for the nearest latrine. Oh, hear me, children, the day of the magazine featuring Farley, Smith, Lovecraft, Campbell, et al. is gone, yea, gone. We are now in the Dark Ages of the days when we get material by Fred Floopgruber, Milton Mishiginah, Ambrose Barse, and other non-entities whose material is printed in preference to that of the pros simply because *they are fans*, and *it is frowned upon to run the work of pros*!

When I ran an issue of *Science Fantasy Bulletin* featuring a number of well-known pros, I was flayed alive by numerous "old-guard" fans, who summed up their revulsion thusly: "Granted it was a fine issue, still, you are publishing a *fan*zine, and don't want too many pros therein. It should never be that a pro has precedence over a FAN..." The word "fan" carried with it awed tones much akin to those used when speaking of F.D.R. down South or of speaking of Jehovah, anywhere. Here is a boldfaced argument that tells me to reject the material of pros, in lieu of that from fans...*even though it is dreadfully inferior*! Their only redeeming feature is that the poor dumb creadle-heads are fans! *This* is an advantage.

But back to the fanzines.

Here we have fanzines that are sloppy imitations of something or other the prototype of which is not even discernable. In the old days, the gay young fan would ditto up a cheap imitation of *Wonder Stories* (and I have seen some that were almost exact replicas, even to the Science Fiction League emblem and the amateur-Paul cover and the other tricks that Papa Hugo used to use—used to use?—when he was in fine mettle) and send it around. But to compensate for these sterile attempts at heroworship, there were such magazines as *Spaceways*, and the fanzine (title on tip of tongue but unremembered at moment) which featured the *Cosmos* serial by numerous well-known pro authors. (A SIDELIGHT: one of the chapters of the *Cosmos* serial—the chapter by S. Fowler Wright—was sent to Lester del Rey when he was still editing *Space*, by agent Forrest J. Ackerman with a note stating that few people had seen it, so why didn't Lester go ahead and buy it from Forry and run it as a new story. Needless to say del Rey bounced the thing so hard, Forry's still applying Band Aids.) But nowadays, when we hit a slush-pile like *Boo!* (though the editor of same is a reasonably good friend of mine), we can cast about, and find but three or four others to compensate. Those compensators are the ones I set aside at the beginning of this column, and no, modesty does not forbid me to mention my own publication. *Boo!, Confusion, Reason, Brevizine,* and several dozens of others all issue forth sporadically bearing with them

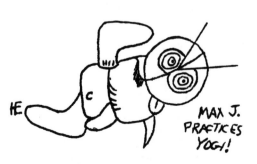

MAX J. PRACTICES YOGI!

seeds of ferment that bode ill for the fanzines field, as such. Each bad fanzine drags down three good ones a notch. And since we are nearly scraping bottom already, it is one helluva climb up out of the slush barrel for the conscientious editor. Mags like *Psychotic*, *Vega*, *Fan-To-See*, and a few others, the new crop, are making names for themselves simply because they are borrowing concepts and inclinations from the "old style" of doing things. And they're doing it well. The mags I've mentioned in this column are all on my reading list. Even some of the ones named in a deprecatory manner (such as *Confusion* and *Boo!*) I find enjoyable. But at the same time recognize their possible danger.

How to resolve the problem? Uh-uh; don't ask me. Campbell says that sixty percent of the problem is posing the problem, the other forty is solving it. I've done 60% of your work—now go to it, you multi-toed fanzine editors. Results! Results! he cried in falsetto.

APPRAISAL II: Phil Farmer is a sick writer.

While talking several months ago with a fellow, our conversation wandered to Phillip José Farmer and his works. We both concurred that Farmer is a sick author.

His work is almost always darkly tainted with sexual overtones or psychological maladjustments that make for uneasy reading during the perusal of his yarns. Such stories as "Mother" (probably the most sickening story, insofar as content goes, I've ever read) and his latest at this writing, "Strange Compulsion" in *Science Fiction Plus* point perturbed fingers at a serious deficiency in Farmer's writing. While having had but the most pleasant of relations with Farmer during our brief meetings, I must still speak as an objective observer and as a science fiction reader, and comment that I've yet to read a Farmertale in which there wasn't some basic themeology use with foundations grounded in either sexual identification, abnormal psychology, or perverted ideals.

Conclusion: Phil Farmer is a sick writer. His work is sick. It turns my stomach. Phil...see a psychiatrist, quick. You can write—but not *this*!

APPRAISAL III: Good lord in heaven! What I merely tolerated before, and watched with mild apprehension has turned to an amok monster that has scared me more witless than my usual amount in the last two days. There have been four new science fiction magazines issued in the last two months, and I've just come to realize that the staggering total of magazines is not only enough to collapse the present science fictional market, but to permanently corrupt the entire field. Migawd! Can't a man bring out a decent stf mag without the thousand and one leeches in the field leaping on his back, digging in their editorial fangs and sucking out his circulatory blood? Where is this "bright new attitude" of the stf editor? All I can see are a madly scrabbling batch of filthy hucksters imitating the originators, imitating the imitators, and imitating the imitators of imitators! I am sickened. I see here *Orbit Science Fiction*, *Science Fiction Stories*, *Science Stories*, *Cosmos Science Fiction*, and forty others which to me can show no real reason for existence. Here is an earnest and sincerely heartfelt appeal to those money-grubbing slugs in New York. Lads, either get out—or tear your damn throats out! But make it quick...I'm running out of money.

APPRAISAL IV: Palmer, you shifty devil. You are a genius, RAP. There is no argument there, but when you give a big cock-and-bull story to the fans about why *Other Worlds* folded and you started *Science Stories* and took over *Universe* (which was folding with the second issue), instead of telling them that you wanted out from under your distributor, American News, why then I feel slightly aggravated. Why didn't you tell the readers to look on their copies of *OW* and see the letters "ANC," and then to look on the new *Universe* and *SciStories* and see the lovely little "K" that signifies either Kable or Klein News, depending on where you live. Why not fess up and admit that ANC was sucking you dry with lousy distribution, Ray lad? Why not admit that by issuing *two* sft zines, bi-monthly, you get a dandy legal loophole insofar as income taxes are concerned. Why not tell the fans all that, Ray? Hmmm? Oh, I see, you want them to think there's a paper shortage and that you are trying new and dynamic directions in stf editing. Well, if that's how you want to work, then okay by me, sir. The word for *your* type of editor is under "H" in the dictionary, with Webster pronouncing it hi-po-crit. Bye, Ray.

BUT I GHENGHIS KHAH'T HELP IT: which is one dickens of a pun to pull on you folks who've been so nice to me to listen to my inane opinions. But I had to devise some clever way to end this fiasco, and since I'm pooped a-plenty, I suppose this is it. Comments are always welcomed, laudatory or otherwise. But if you were thinking of otherwise, I just might mention that I've been contemplating something Jack Harness wrote about in his farcial "Slaves of Null-A." In it, I got mad at someone, and mailed myself to them disguised as a packet of chicken noodle soup. Beware! Mrs. Grass isn't the only one who has...

The Annals of Aardvark
May 1953

CHAPTER 1: The Entrance

C'mon in won't you? You can sit right down there in that rocking chair. Oh! You saw the sign on the door and wanted to ask me about Aardvark, did you? Well, I guess I'm the best person to tell you about him since I was with him from the moment he entered the country. Do you want to hear from there or from the real beginning? Well, okay, I'll tell you about the start when he met the Valkyries.

You see Aardvarks can live only in the warmest places. So, when the Aardvark got lost in the Swiss Alps, he was very uncomfortable. Don't ask me how an Aardvark got to the Swiss Alps or what he was doing there in the first place. He's never told anyone, except maybe the Valkyries.

Anyhow, stumbling around in the freezing cold, he got lost; but good. Just as he was about to give up and say farewell cruel world, he stumbled upon an ice crypt. Stumbled? He ran into it and knocked out two teeth.

This crypt which was set in the side of one of the glaciers was not an ordinary one, for frozen within its icy walls, rent free, were two Valkyries and a large elephant. Even the elephant was unusual. He was the sole owner (the Valkyries obviously had no use for one!) of a handsome brown handlebar moustache, nicely waxed and glistening.

The Aardvark, who was inquisitive as are all great men, strolled up to the ice crypt as nonchalantly as a freezing Aardvark could, and dying of hunger, put forth an exploratory tongue and licked the ice. To his amazement, the ice was lemon flavored. Wait a minute, I'll tell you why it was lemon flavored, but first let me tell you what happened.

Knowing full well the consequences of licking open this age-old ice pack, but racked with hunger, the Aardvark proceeded to lick open the crypt. After several minutes of lightning like licking, the Aardvark sated his hunger and in the process freed the Valkyries.

The Valkyries were forever grateful and proceeded to show the Aardvark this by bursting into a Wagnerian opera, complete with flowing braids.

After the preceding formality had been dispensed with, introductions went around and the Aardvark found out the fact, which is of practically no use to anyone, that the Valkyries' names were Olga and Ketanya Schwartz. Very old lineage, this name. The elephant, who had been sitting by looking very bored about the whole thing, was named Rubin.

The Valkyries, it seems, were delivering a package of lemon flavored Jell-O to the cook in Valhalla and, en route, had gotten frozen in the ice. The elephant was their mode of conveyance since all the good horses had a day off and went to the people races at Lowaleah.

The Aardvark heard all of this in a rather detached way, for you know most Aardvarks can neither talk, write, nor understand human language... The Valkyries, who perceived this deficiency, were contemplating giving the Aardvark some of their Valkyrie Local Number 86112 Magic, Pat. Pending, when the recipient in question suddenly turned a lovely shade of aquamarine, shivered, and dropped over, frozen solid. This solved the problem very effectively. They worked their second-hand magic on the fellow and when he awoke...! Well, there was as a complete change in him. This was the exit of Aardvark, boy nothing, and the entrance of Cassius Quagmire Aardvark, man of the world.

Chapter 2: Mass Exodus

After the Valkyries had revived Cassius with the aid of a bouquet consisting of a quartet of red flowers in liquid form, they placed him and themselves upon the back of the elephant Rubin, who it was found was permanently grounded after three or four thousand years of disuse, and proceeded to the almost obscure town of Eeahohaheee, Switzerland, where they intended to settle down.

But the people of the town upon seeing the apparition of a large elephant with a moustache carrying two beautiful girls and a strange animal, wanted to burn the Aardvark and his companions at the stake thinking them a figment of their imaginations.

The elephant did not care for this in the least and rearing back on his hind legs proceeded to tell the townsfolk so, much to their dismay. In large groups they immediately depopulated the Swiss village.

Cassius, the Aardvark, finding himself alone in the middle of a deserted town with a mustachioed elephant and two Valkyries decided that here they were not appreciated, and made preparations for leaving the country.

In a deserted haberdashery he found a fine, warm English tweed, a top hat, white gloves, a white bow tie, and a pair of lavender earmuffs, which he quickly donned. The elephant was equipped with a can of moustache wax and a muffler, while the Schwartz sisters doffed their filmy négligé type goddess gowns and donned two lovely business suits.

Then, well clothed and happy, the elephant replaced his traveling companions upon his back, and calmly swam the Atlantic Ocean to arrive at the United States of America, where the Aardvark's appearance was destined to cause a stir and tremor in the daily life of every American.

Chapter 3: "...It's a Bargain"

A warning of the thing to sweep the country shortly was evidenced when the mustachioed elephant Rubin came lumbering through the water in the New York Harbor. People from miles around who got wind of the news (he was a very smelly elephant) rushed to the docks to watch, or to climb to the tops of buildings with binoculars. And when Rubin climbed ashore on Ellis Island, the city was thrown into a panic.

It seems that Cassius began conferring at once with two of the immigration officers about entrance into the country. This was flatly refused by the officials, who cited a weak clause in the handbook which excluded all uncivilized beings, and anyone could see that Cassius was uncivilized—whoever heard of wearing lavender earmuffs with an English tweed.

When his traveling companions heard this, they were all for hurling the immigration officers head first into ye olde New Yawk Harbor.

Right about there is where I came in. Yeah, good old Charlie Smirtz, that's me. I had been waiting on the island for a shipload of animals from Africa and being a producer of some renown, saw the latent possibilities in the appearance of these, and I use the term loosely, people. I had just finished a show on Broadway that had run three years and was just getting together an animal circus to tour the country. But when I saw this Aardvark in an English tweed with a top hat, tie, and ivory-topped cane, a moustached elephant wearing a muffler, and two of the most gawjus dames in the world, I knew that this was something a little unusual. I was sure of it when I saw that the Aardvark was wearing lavender earmuffs.

Sauntering casually over to where the Aardvark and his companions were sitting, I introduced myself, and in a low voice related to them the fact that if they would consent to signing a contract, I would personally see that they were inside the country before morning. The Aardvark gives me the cold eye at first and then says, "If you promise, and write it out in this contract that we are not to appear in any sideshow type things, we might consent."

Before the fellow could twitch his short brown tail, I had pulled out my Foster pen that writes under water, air, ink, blood, and money, and was writing in the clause he mentioned. Then he signed the contract, and so commenced the partnership of Smirtz, Aardvark, Schwartz, and Rubin, Inc.

Chapter 4: The Carbuncle Voyage

After the signing of the contract, Cassius and his companions retired to the harbor to wait till I had made the arrangements. Late that night, very late (about five o'clock), a small tug pulled up to the island and out came one Hawser Dawson. I can truthfully say that Hawser is the moldiest looking animal ever to set foot upon dry land. Or wet water, for that matter. He is so filthy that his clothes stand up by themselves when he takes them off at night. And the smell! WHEWWW!! Hawser Dawson smells like Mrs. Murphy didn't get home with the eggs in time. He is dirty, smelly, and dumb besides, but he is loyal and one of the best tugboat captains that ever tripped on a two-inch line.

We had arranged to get the Aardvark and his buddies into the country under cover but I had forgotten to mention to Hawser how big the group was. When Hawser saw the elephant he almost fainted. His ship, which was as leaky as Stalin's head, wouldn't carry that load. It could hardly carry Hawser himself. So we arranged to hang the Aardvark and the elephant under the ship while the Valkyries and I rode upstairs.

But not only did Dawson get paid twice as much as he should have, he wanted the Aardvark and Rubin the elephant to work their way in. He whispered something to Cassius and Rubin and then came aboard. When the elephant and our hero were slung under the ship, the leaky tub sank so low into the water that it was wetter on the bridge than it was under the ship. We got under way shortly and as we sailed around under cover of darkness we heard a weird sound. It was a systematic metallic whonking under the boat. When we asked Dawson what the noise was, he told us that the Aardvark and Rubin were working their way over by cleaning barnacles off the bottom of the tugboat with their teeth. I almost fainted when I heard this. Our future star, the brightest new personality in years...scraping barnacles! Oh no!

After breaking a steel pipe over Dawson's head, we got the Aardvark into the ship and started chipping the remnants of his work from his bicuspids. It was about this time that we got into the small dock that Hawser had told us would be waiting. We dragged the slightly defunct sea captain out of the ship, got Rubin out from under and proceeded to enter the United States of America, which as you know has since been renamed by some people, the United States of Aardvark. One of the reasons is because of what happened in the Drunken Cockroach Nightclub. Oh was that a queer night. It happened on the same evening we got into the States...

Chapter 5: In the Drunken Cockroach

We got the Aardvark settled quickly in a hotel near the center of town and then decided to go out and eat someplace. Hawser Dawson wanted to go along till he got his money and since he wanted it in cash and the banks didn't open till the next day we decided to let him tag along. There was but one stipulation: that he take a bath. This almost broke Stinky's heart but he consented and when he met us in the lobby a few hours later, he was (as he termed it) "disgustingly filthy clean."

Rubin was looking quite elegant in a rented tux which was a size sixty-seven. The Schwartz girls were absolutely ravishing in their two evening gowns that were strapless, hemless, backless, topless, bottomless, frontless, and with a plunging neckline.

But the really dashing one was Cassius Q. Aardvark. He was

decked out in a conservative green and red suit with a yellow tie, spats, a cane, top hat, and the perennial lavender earmuffs. We could never understand it but the newspapers said the next day that about fifty cases of color blindness and shock were brought into the hospital raving about an Aardvark with a top hat and earmuffs.

That was really a queer night. We started out at the Stork Club. Sherm Billingsley had gotten wind of the Aardvark and had a special room reserved with a wall knocked out for the elephant Rubin. The men were practically fawning all over the Schwartz Valkyries, who calmly broke champagne bottles over their heads and continued to stay by their dear pal, the Aardvark. After we had gotten well placed I looked at the Aardvark. He was holding sway like a royal Sultan, complete with dancing girls. The young blade was surrounded by the chorus line and was having a rough time with them. But he had eyes only for the Schwartz sisters. They sat there exchanging guttural sounds.

After we got finished at the Stork we took in rapid succession the Mocambo, the 21, 22, 23, 24, and 25 Clubs, the Noire Pansy Club, and the Hi, Low, Top, and Homburg Hat Clubs.

About nine o'clock we were just about pooped out when we noticed that we had lost Hawser someplace. It was quite a relief to us as he had poured the contents of a potted palm over himself at the Noire Pansy Club to make himself feel more at home and he had begun to reacquire the odor that was peculiar only to his body.

It was then that Cassius remarked, "Look at the neighborhood we're in. This is lower than low."

Truer than true were his words. We were in a neighborhood that looked like the inside of a shell-shocked oyster shell. We were surrounded by broken down houses and buildings that looked as though they had been old when Moxie's Army was chewing on rattles. At the end of the street that we were on was a building that was a little better; just a little. By better, I mean it was standing. There was a sign over the door that proceeded to tell us in no uncertain terms that this was the "Drunken Cockroach Nightclub."

I was all for turning back as was Cassius Q., but the Valkyries, Olga and Ketanya, who had consumed a great deal of wine (they learned how in Valhalla, they told us), ran on ahead and without a backward hiccough vanished into the rickety building which threatened at any moment to fall on their heads.

With a shrug to the gods of Chance, Rubin, Cassius, and I proceeded to the Spirit Hostelry, or as you choose, beer parlor.

The inside of the Drunken Cockroach was worse than the outside. It looked like a nightmare by Dali on a night when he had run out of brushes and had started using his feet.

The bar, which ran across the back of the smoke-filled room, was of a seasick green, the walls a burnt umber tinged with beige. The floor was ornamented with a five-pointed star that showed several crawly type animals such as the kind that "go bump in the night." They were of various hues and were, in all, quite sickening. The bartender was the worst. A small sign above the bar related the fact that he was Oliver Absinthe. He was not only repulsive, he was nauseating: a large bald head encased in folds of pink flesh, surmounting the largest gut stomach bay window in the country, excepting Rubin's. He was wearing an apron that showed the demise of many a martini. There were also spaghetti, dirt, milk, coffee, and gravy stains on the apron, and a group of green blotches that I couldn't quite place. It looked like the remains of last week's spinach.

Have you ever heard a sick Hippo tell you about his operation? Well, if not, try to imagine how it would sound, since that was what this fellow's voice sounded like. "What's ya pleasure?" he said.

"Nothing much," I answered, looking for a quick way to get out if it was needed.

We seated ourselves in a booth next to the Valkyries who were fast at work guzzling beer. Rubin just stood with one foot on the brass rail which, at the application of his weight, bent. He ordered another double double scotch and in one gulp downed it. It was then that the elephant began screeching in an unelephantlike way and kicking himself in his more than ample posterior. We started shaking him by the trunk and asked him what the trouble was and he yelled that the last drink was one too many. He was seeing pink people.

After this outburst I returned to the booth to see that the Aardvark was gone. My attempts at locating him were halted suddenly by the screaming of another person. It seems as though that evening was open season on howling. The person yelling was Oliver Absinthe, the bartender, who was yelling at Cassius who was in turn yelling and alternately beating with his fists and a cuspidor a slot machine that was not acting in the way Cassius expected it to. With a resounding howl the machine exploded showering colored lights, nickels, pieces of wire, and an Aardvark at me. The last was caught by Ketanya Schwartz in one hand while downing a beer with the other. Absinthe was jumping up and down behind his seasick green bar while the rather shady looking patrons were scrambling for the nickels.

Absinthe, who had been systematically withdrawing each strand of hair from his chest (his head was bald), let loose a barrage of verbal abuse that even singed my ears. Besides that, he let loose a string of whiskey bottles that sailed across the room and felled, one at a time, the clientele on the opposite side. The bodies began piling up as Oliver the bartender became not only bald on his head, but upon his barrel chest also. I for one dove for safety under the table, and there was pleasantly surprised to find the half-pickled Olga Schwartz still swilling spirits. I raised my head in time to see the Aardvark swinging across the nearly ruined room on the trunk of Rubin, who was sitting in the middle of the floor hitting himself and repeating, "Go away, go away." Giving out a sound like Tarzan with the gout, he flew through the murky smoke-filled air and with a sidearm that would do Bob Feller credit, hit the still-bellowing bartender a resounding clunk in the cranium. Absinthe fell like a poled ox.

By this time there was much yelling and hollering by everyone within a radius of two blocks. In the distance we heard the mournful wail that signals the entrance of the blue-coated gendarmes. With a significant look we aroused Rubin, whose moustache had begun to droop sadly, climbed upon his back, and amidst the clatter and crash of beer bottles, escaped the "Drunken Cockroach Nightclub." Like I said, what a night!

Chapter 6: None So Blind as Love

These were the times. The good times that I still remember as I rock back and forth before my fire. Eh? Whassat? Oh, yeah, less ruminating and more expostulating. Heh, that's a good one, sonny, but don't be gettin' flip with me...old Smirtz can still tan the hide off'n any young whippersnapper like you.

Well, anyhow, I had been making plans to put Cassius and his band into a supra-super-colossal extravaganza that would out Florenz Ziegfeld. It was about six months after that mad night at the Cockroach that rehearsals were over, the show was prepared, the public waited with bated breath and fish-hooks to see what had been the most highly touted production in a decade.

Then that night.

I can remember it as if it were twelve years ago. (As a matter of fact, it WAS twelve years ago.) The marquees blazoned their messages to the crowd that had formed a line *fourteen* times around the block in front of the Garden. New York had turned out en masse. And, as I said, those marquees!

THE AARDVARK FOLLIES
Starring CASSIUS Q. AARDVARK
with RUBIN, OLGA and KETANYA SCHWARTZ,
MILTON BERLE, LAWRENCE OLIVIER,
LIONEL BIRDBATH
and others

an extravaganza to
out-ganza all extras!!
STANDING ROOM ONLY

How d'y' like that? SRO signs up, *and we hadn't even opened yet*!

Well, when that curtain rose and the Aardvark came out on the backs of seventy raging rhinoceriii, the crowd went into fits. And when the Schwartz girls danced the dance of the 8½ x 11 Kleenex, you could have sworn that the rafters would buckle. And when Rubin did his imitation of the President (oh that imitation of *Mamie*!), the Garden sounded as though 12 billion Zulus were singing, "Tide's in, Smirtz out."

Thirteen weeks went by with two shows a day except when Cassy got tired, and the money was rolling in. We had to save a box seat each night for Impelliterri, otherwise the cops would have closed us down. It wasn't exactly blackmail, I don't blame him a bit, that was one helluva show.

However, all good things must come to an end.

We had signed on a pair of kids named...uh...what in the...oh yeah—yeah, that's it, Martin, for some fill-in stuff 'tween acts (We had to let 'em go eventually. We found 'em carrying on with one of the hatcheck girls name of Monroe, or something. Oh well.) and Cass had taken off a week to go down to Monte Carlo for some sun and air. That year, the rage of the Riviera were two three-headed girls named Sally Louise

Lee Munglefootz and Gertrude Alice Roberta Hitslongle (they called them SLL and GAR for short), and when they saw Cassius...

Well, it went on for three gay, mad days till I sent a wire back to New York to tell Olga and Ketanya to get down to Le Ville de Mazuma to save Cass-boy from what might develop into a septangle.

SLL and GAR were entertaining Cass at a party one night, drinking borscht from his sneakers, when who should drop in through a skylight from a DC-6 but the Schwartz sisters who immediately began laying about them with a pair of two-handed broadswords. Fifteen minutes and ninety gallons of blood later the place was cleared of all sentience save Cass, myself, the Schwartz girls, and a drunken cockroach (something familiar about that boy) who immediately staggered to the seashore, fell in, and was poisoned to death.

Cassius, basking in such munificent attention, and also regaling himself with the beauty of the two girls, immediately realized how unhappy he really was in civilization. He pleaded on bended bodies for forgiveness, and upon being received warmly by Olga and Ketanya, made plans for his leaving "culture."

I didn't try to stop him.

What would'a been the use? I'd made enough to retire, Cass had seen the World, Rubin had been adopted by some destitute family named DuPont who wanted a house pet, and all in all, the only drawback was that I hated to see him go.

But finally he chartered a plane (something about a sacred cow I believe) and took off back to where he felt was home with the two Schwartz Valkyries.

Yep, that's the last anyone ever saw of 'em. That is, till now. Huh? Where are they? And what am I doin' here? Well, you see I didn't figger on taxes after the show...and I was broke in two months. That's what I'm doin' here. Eh? Where are they?

Well, just ste-ep right up, ladeez and gennulmen, for onny twenny-fi' cents I'm gonna show you a real, authentic, forsure aardvark and two girls frozen into a block of lemon flavored ice, right here in the heart of the Swiss...

Why I Hate Lynn Hickman, Boy Fan

March 1953

I don't hate Lynn Hickman, but it sounded good when I was looking so feverishly for a title for this abortion. Now I have a title and I'm bound to go ahead and turn all fandom against me. For everyone loves Lynn Hickman. He's a stout fellow. Actually he isn't stout, he's more or less thin with hair on his head. I don't hold that against him—lots of fellows have foliage atop their craniums.

Carole Hickman is the one I really hate, because she caused me aggravation this afternoon when I kept tilting the pin ball machine in the Quatt Wunkery downtown, and I couldn't get the damned machine to stop sneering at me. It seems that this particular machine hated me. But I got him...I clipped him right on the chops. Bashed him one on his glass encased head, the varlet. Later they had to put an out of order sign on him. What a buffoon that machine was.

The Long Episode
March-April 1953

"When, in 2037, The United Governments of Terra banned all 'lunatic fringe' organizations, on the grounds that they were, 'Detrimental to the mental level of the enlightened peoples of Terra,' the Amalgamated Science Fiction Fen of Other Orbs (ASFOO) trundled each other into one monstrous spaceship called the *Star Bem* and with their own screwball hierarchy known only as 'BNF,' went off somewhere into the star-flecked vastness of space, never to be seen again. As this was in the same approximate era as the discovery of the Youth Restoratives and Elixirs, their departure went relatively unnoticed. However, we can now look back and see the good luck which it was that caused them to leave Terra and..."

A RETROSPECTIVE ANALYSIS
OF MANKIND'S STRUGGLES (1942–2067)
by Thomas Brokman
(Simon & Birdbath, New New York, 2068, 7752pp.)

episode the first:
Destination and Destiny

Below them in the waist-high blue grass there was a whispering of the mountain winds. All about them as they sat beneath the Kopi-trees there was a calling and humming as though a million voices from some limitless past were beckoning to them. They let their thoughts slide out of focus. Back they went to the first days of the arrival on Tucker. They'd named it that out of sentimental respect. Tuck had been the only one the Youth Restoratives missed. All the others, Hoffx, Keasler, Vick, Venable, all of them, they'd had their shots and the youth had come back to their lined and seamed faces, they were able to lead their children to the promised land.

Oh, the first years had been difficult. There were cases of unrest and minor mutiny. There were those who never should have been brought along, of course, like Degler and Beale, but that couldn't be helped. They were in good standing and they *did* fall into the category whether the Foundling Fathers liked it or not, as they obviously didn't.

That first year, with the huts and the scrabbling for food and the foolish, foolish wasting of time on establishing cities when they all knew deep in their hearts that the Libraries and the Museums and the ConSites were the really important things to be getting on with.

There were no deaths that first year except...

Yes, now that they thought back, there was one death.

A young fellow named Ellison; making something of a name for himself, he was. He got his right in his own backyard as a matter of fact. The way the story went he tripped over a red birdbath or something of the sort. But progress and the Fen had gone on.

In the primeval days the pack was the most important. In the medieval period it was the clan, and in the pre- and post-atomic era it was the culture. But here, on Tucker, there was nothing more essential, nothing for which they would fight more than...the Fen.

The dreamers under the tree thought back to the times when the first party had gone into the swamps. Into the Red Swamp and the Green and the Black Swamps. They had, in their youthful exuberance named them Prodom, Nirvana, and Shaver Swamps respectively. They remembered those five staunch explorers Korshak, Eshbach, Evans, Bloch, and ol' Ditky who had gone out and blazed paths through the clinging multi-colored hells to stumble upon the valley that nestled down between the jungles on three sides and the Moskowitz chain on the fourth. They had come back out with tales that thrilled the expedition to its very core. They had packed their belongings, torn down the rude huts they had established and moved off in a long line through the cloying dampness of the vari-hued muck.

Three weeks march brought them out on the edge of the plateau, the valley stretching out in magnificent array before and below them, a green, grassy bowl with the many-colored suns of the Pleiades shining down upon its verdant glory.

They had taken the valley over immediately. Work and more work had followed upon the heels of labor and more labor. And now...one hundred years later they could look out over that valley—and beyond, for the Fen had cleared away the stinking growths of the jungles and even, in their boundless enthusiasm, moved the Moskowitz chain back till it rested upon the shore of the Ackerman covering nearly half of Tucker—and see the shining spires of New Toronto glinting gaily in the reflected glare of those same suns which had shown down upon their rejuvenated elders.

This was the world.

This was the way it had been for the last hundred years. No wars, no sickness, no pestilence. Minor feuds, yes, for they were an integral part of Fandom, but even the feuds were carried out with a sort of mock solemnity that bespoke the good will harbored by one and all toward each other.

The dreamers beneath the tree cursed inwardly at the circumstances which now forced them to make use of...

They looked off toward the far reaches of New Toronto, off on the other side of the bowl that encompassed their capitol they saw the grim outline of that battered hulk that had brought them to this paradise and would now most likely carry them away. They cursed again, this time openly. The N3F had ruled they must return to Earth to reclaim their heritage...and so they must. Orders were seldom given on Tucker, unless it was obvious that such rules *must* be given. But this was a rule that most of the Fen did not like. It meant going back to face the coldly unreceptive world that had once cast them away as a dead and useless or abominable idea is cast away. It had ridiculed and persecuted them... and now it held what the Officers called their Heritage.

Ish rose to his feet, brushing idly at his jumper to remove the damp grass, "Come on, let's go see Venable," he snapped, heading down the slope toward the slideway that inched its way across the sward beneath them. The other four arose and trundled after him, leaving their imprints on the damp grassy slope.

episode the second:
The Elder Disputation

The long hall stretched away practically out of sight. Massive white pillars upheld the multi-frescoed walls with their detailed murals. The five Fen stared aghast (though they'd seen them a hundred times) at each separate picture signed with the most famous names of antiquity:

"Emsh," "Finlay," "Cartier," "Bok," "Bergey," all monstrous reproductions of both reprint and original artwork, some brought from the mother planet and some completed in this new haven.

The stately door slid into the wall at their approach, the faint whispering of it as it retired on its bearings adding a touch of reality to this fantastic place.

They entered and sat down on the five relaxers placed facing a blank wall on which a three-dimensional colortone wavered and danced. Just as suddenly as the door had opened for them, the wall rose and revealed the seated N3F Officers—the Council of Elders.

Ish and his companions suppressed a smile. Though they had seen the trick of the sliding wall a multitude of times, they could not get over the Elders' flair for the ridiculously dramatic.

"You wish to dispute the decision," asked the one at the head of the table.

"Yes, Venable, we wish to dispute this proclamation which will force us to leave a hundred-year-old sanctuary for the dubious pleasure of returning to that demented planet some five hundred light-years away," said Ish, his young face breaking into a worried frown.

The Elder arose and, nodding to his fellow officers, paced toward the front of the dais, picking his words carefully as he went: "One hundred and twelve years ago, we were bodily thrown off Earth, told to get the Hell away and not to return. What happened to us was a matter of no concern to the peoples of Earth. We came here, over 500 light-years away and started afresh. We have built a highly advanced culture, much more stable and more enjoyable to us all than the one we left. But nonetheless, we left with a black mark against us, with the hoots and catcalls of the human race at our backs.

"Through all these one hundred years that has been the one driving force of the Fen to correct the demerit, to regain our rightful place in society—back on Earth!"

LsberE leaped to his feet beside Ish, "But *why* do we have to go to that sinkhole? In my opinion we'd be better off to let Earth and its peoples think we'd perished. Besides, how do we know that there is even any Earth there anymore? Even going at the speed we attained on our way here, man should have caught up with us over fifty years ago. What if they killed each other off...or what if they were invaded by another race...or what if...?"

NanG, sitting quietly on the dais till then, said "Obviously, something happened on Earth. But just the same, we must get to Earth and make them acknowledge our heritage...make them once more accept us as members of the human race! Besides, we owe them a form of allegiance. They are our brothers. Perhaps we can help them. It is our duty..."

"The Hell you say!" cried English, jumping from the relaxer, "We owe them nothing! They laughed at us from the day Gernsback and Campbell (there was a faint wind of reverence at mention of the names) got the field underway. They laughed at us even when we left. *They're probably still laughing!*"

The talk bantered back and forth for hours with, eventually, the major portion of the Fen trailing into the Beatley and standing in the huge reception chamber to listen. For this concerned them all. Vitally.

Eventually, as the hours dragged by, the discussion tapered down to the conclusion that perhaps the whole Fen should not go, but a delegation be sent to re-introduce itself to Earth, estimate what was wrong that man had not followed the Fen to the stars, and finally re-establish communications.

It was decided and the discussion blossomed anew, for though the individual was so devoted to the Fen that he would not let the entire culture pick itself up and return to Earth, by himself he wanted to see the lone moon of their birth and the smoking cities and the blue skies and...

After lengthy deliberation it was decided that a crew of twenty, representing every phase of Fandom, would be sent in a new ship to be built after the standards of the *Star Bem* but with many improvements and additions that would enable more speed and more accuracy of astrogation.

The expedition was to be led by Elder Fabun, with a hand-picked crew of Fen that would cover not only every phase of spaceship control, but every phase of fanning.

LsberE was included to provide the biting satire which made him the culture's George Bernard Shaw, Hoff was sent along as a representative of humor in fandom, $quires went as a disciple of the deep concept in fandom, and Walter @wls went as a carrier of genial good-naturement. There were fifteen others, all picked for his or her outstanding trait or talent...and they went prepared.

It seemed as though it were centuries later when the *Ootpla! II* stood in its cradle at Macauley Spaceport, nose pointed heavenward, proud bulk poised as if to leap out into the green-hued vastness that surrounded Tucker and thence into the black and eternal night of space, bound for the mother planet: Earth.

The passengers kissed their loved ones, waved goodbye to the milling throng which contained almost every soul on the face of Tucker.

Then without a backward glance , the assembled explorers stepped onto the plasticine slideway and in a moment were whisked inside the gaping maw of the *Ootpla! II.*

A cautionary bleep on the spaceport foghorns and the crowd moved back behind the transparent bunkers. From somewhere there came the preliminary thunder of the atomic motors warming. Suddenly a burst of livid flame shot out around the base of the ship and in an instant it was poised on a thin obelisk of flame, and then...

It roared out of sight into the green sky.

episode the third:
Energy Build-Up

A metal fish swam through a stream of special darkness. The myriad tell-tale resplendencies of the far-off nebulas giving the scene an atmosphere of ethereal beauty. Inside the ship the twenty emissaries to Earth spent their time in routine inspection and re-inspection of the ship, and their off-duty hours in the usual fanpractices. Over thirteen hundred one-shot fanzines were issued inside the shell of the *Ootpla! II* during that long saunter back through the densities of the void.

Down in the engine room, HonE Wood, Tucker's most renowned rocket jockey, one of the few Fen discovered who possessed latent esp powers, was applying her innate familiarity with machinery to making the *Ootpla! II*'s guts operate according to Tucker.*

Wood had been one of the lesser BNF on Tucker till one day she found that "Just by sticking my hands in and wiggling 'em," she could

---

* An interesting bit of terminology, "According to Tucker." Aside from the fact that the planet colonized by The Fen was named after the great man since he had often been parliamentarian of many conventions, the saying, "According to Hoyle," taken after a game expert of the 20th century was altered accordingly...

put to right any machinery gone haywire. A study into her mental processes located a most startling ability on her part to "feel" when machinery of a complex nature was out of whack.

Because of that ability, she had gone unchallenged in her application of Chief Mech on the *Ootpla! II*'s journey.

Her small world in the hold of the ship was one of utter neatness and homogeneity. She was well-known for her neat-as-the-proverbial-pin cleanliness, and the engine room seemed to sparkle with an amazing brilliance only attained by the most discerning women.

Upstairs, on the thirty decks, The Fen wended their multitudinous ways, an electric tension in the air, for no one even dared guess at what awaited them on Earth...though they all *did* guess. Incessantly.

The weeks passed slowly, yet rapidly.

The wall annunciator rasped accusingly. A scarlet glow, bloodily insistent, suffused the entire ship. Relays closed. Knife switches slashed home. The PA system bleated monotonously, yet urgently, "Situation Scarlet! Situation Scarlet! Situation Scarlet! Situat..."

All through the ship bulkhead doors were slamming on pneumatic sealers, the Fen on-duty were slamming their way to their assigned posts and the sleeping shift was tumbling frantically from its bunks. Pandemonium was rampant. No one knew what was going on.

With stunning force a voice split the mad rumble of sounds into a ragged jigsaw puzzle of noise, silencing the near-rioting crowd: "This is HonE. I'm in the antechamber to the Pile Room. We've developed a clogged-up reactor chamber. One of the caddie rods slipped out and we're building up potential like interest on a three-year loan. Somebody's going to have to go in there and shove the damned thing back in. And, oh yes...come on down here, I've got a surprise for you."

En masse the Fen filled the elevators and within minutes were clustered together in the huge antechamber of the reactor room, with its burnished metal walls, unbroken save for the wide, glassite portals through which those in the antechamber could see the monstrous and bloated bulk of the cadmium-rod generating pile that powered the *Ootpla! II.*

On a small raised platform affair near the front of the room, HonE Wood, rakish captain's hat snapped over to one side of her head, stood grasping by the scruff of his jumper a young boy, who was frantically squirming to break out of her grip.

Elder Fabun, the only member of the N3F high council who allowed himself to age somewhat, lending the impression of extreme age, strode purposefully up to the raised platform, his long, white beard swaying in unison with the movement of his lean body.

"What is the meaning of this, DavIsh?" the elder addressed the still-squirming youngster, who seemed to shrink in upon himself at the obviously enraged tones of the older man.

A flood of words burst from the youth's mouth, tumbling over each other in a mad rush to be voiced. "I wanted to come along. They told me the quota had been filled and that all the facets of fanning had been selected. They said there wasn't any space for me. I—I just *had* to come along." He seemed as though he were about to burst with the concerted emotions that had spewed forth.

"I found him in one of the mixture rooms under the antechamber," she indicated a circular opening in the floor. "He must have smuggled some food in while we were finishing the ship. He's been down there for weeks. It's a wonder he's still alive. The acceleration must have been murder without a pneumoseat. Got to admit that the kid's got spunk."

DavIsh, the stowaway, starred in unashamed fear of the Elder, who towered above him. When the youth restoratives had been discovered, DavIsh had been the only one who wanted to return to the days of his youth, and consequently had retreated, via the drugs, to the physical and mental attitudinal capacities of a fourteen year old.

The Elder looked down at the boy, his stern visage broken only momentarily by a gleam of admiration that went unseen by even the youth. "You have done a very foolish thing, my boy," he started. "There is only enough food on this ship for..."

He never finished, for suddenly one of the technicians, watching a bank of dials to the side of the platform cried, "Look, the energy's building up to the red line! We'll all go up in a minute!"

HonE Wood let loose of DavIsh and made to enter the radioactivity-filled chamber through the thick, barred door, but three of the Fen near the door, Vick, Hikm&, and Rtrapp, barred her way.

"You're the only good mech on the ship HonE," blurted Ln Hikm&. "You're needed too badly."

"No, I'm dispensable," another burst out.

"I'll go," cried a voice from the rear.

"No, I!"

"I'm the one!"

But no one made to open that death-concealing orifice into the pile room.

The technician by the banks bellowed above the tumult, "We're reaching maximum! There's no time left! The ship's going to explode! It's no use..."

episode the fourth:
Self-Effacement -- A Hero's Death

They stood, paralyzed; waiting, waiting, waiting for the final bit of nuclear reaction that would pile onto the top of the already staggeringly compounded potential and erupt them all into hyperspace, evaporating them into a nova-hot cloud of radioactive dust at the same moment, depriving hyperspace of the pleasure of imploding them into blobs of insensate matter.

they stood...

And suddenly, the stowaway, DavIsh, leaped from the platform and tugged open the dogged valves that kept the huge lead-lined door shut. In an instant he was through, into the radioactively deadly chamber, and faintly, through its bulk they heard the valves snap into place once again...this time with the young boy inside.

As one their gaze turned to the portal in the wall, through which they could see the monster of the pile, towering over the slight figure of the boy, obviously being bombarded with wave after wave of sterilizing, deadly gamma rays!

They watched as he strode across the chamber to the pile.

They stared dumbfounded as he suddenly tottered on his feet and sank to one knee, pushing a hand across his forehead, brushing back the mop of hair that had fallen over it as he stumbled. For a moment it looked as though he would fall there and never get up, but pushing against the metallic floor with both hands, he rose, sweating, and teetered to the pile where the cadmium-rod was dangling uselessly on its chain. The gaping maw of the rod-hole, from which the caddie-rod had skipped, was before him, as he hoisted the ninety lb. bar in his arms and slipping, shoved it into the hole...

Immediately, the dials and gauges on the technician's board registered a marked decrease in the RA level, as the purifyers sped their multitudinous processes to account for the unbelievably high ray content.

"Good God," screamed Hoffχ, her face turning ashen, drawing the attention of the stunned Fen back to the portal, through which they could see the Pile Room.

Inside on the floor, misshapenly sprawled was the body of the young stowaway. Under the tremendous bombardment of the high-velocity radioactivity his body was slowly dematerializing. As they watched, in complete horror, the body began to dissolve, froth, fall in upon itself, and then, in a second...was gone.

Dimly, through a half-conscious haze, the white-faced Elder Fabun heard the women screaming. Out of the corner of his eye he saw that even the strong-constitutioned Chief Mech, Wood, was swaying.

LsberE and Silvrbrg, who had been standing together, pressed the switches which rendered opaque the two close-set portals.

They stood before the great yawning gate of natural space; looking into its well-like depths. Through its multi-faceted brilliance to the rim of the Galaxy. Someone in the rear of the observatory was intoning a deep, heartfelt prayer. And the women cried. And the men stood straight and painfully tall, much too tense, belying their stony silence.

Each bore in his or her mind that final picture of the boy, tottering against the pile, with the ponderous rod in his arms, sweat rolling from his youthfully strained face, the nerves taut in his neck. And the women cried.

Even those to whom a "god" was fallacy, even those who snidely spoke of Ghu and Roscoe as their personal deities, even those...they no longer laughed, and it seemed that a bit of the God-light shone in on them in their bullet-shaped omnibus.

They closed the observatory dome, blocking off the view of normal space. In a few moments the ship shuddered and everyone tossed off a hyperpill and liquid. Many of those who tossed it off did so with the most devastating liquor he could find in the ship.

The last leg of the journey went by without incident. The ship barreled on through hyperspace with its milk-white pallor shot through with sky-blue streaks of lightning. There was less gayety now, for sobriety had touched even the most jocose of the travelers.

Thirteen days out from Earth, if the astrogations were accurate, they switched back to normal space, but few went to look at the many-splendored tapestry of it.

The astrogator, Art Wesley[2], the only mutant that had ever been able to live in fandom, pored over his graphs long into the "night," and only when one of his heads would sleep would the other deign to imbibe coffee or StaveSleep pills. The left head, Kincannon, was the mathematician of the combo, while GreNL, the right head, was the calculator. Together their charts and calculations could be depended upon to be accurate. No one felt pity for the mutant, for his intelligence was so high that most of the other Fen felt somewhat dwarfed by his presence. The only reason he had not been taken into the N3F high council was that an overbudding inferiority complex had been born in him, and to cover it a perpetual air of jocularity surrounded him.

Nonetheless, he was not only respected, but held somewhat in awe. And from that band of extreme individualists, it was indeed an honor.

It was a week out. They had left the Centaurian chains far behind. Ahead, the orb of Sol, lost to their sight for over one hundred years, was blazing like some incandescent lozenge against the jewelers' pad of deep space.

Five days out.

Four days out.

A trio of "days" and "nights" on their titanium coracle was all that separated them from the resting-place of their ancestors' bones.

Two days from Earth and they left the frigid outer planets in the wake of their nuclear tail, and were speeding down upon the redly criss-crossed face of Mars.

Puzzlement surrounded them, and conjecture ran high, for the well-established (when they left) colonies on Mars were gone. Not a trace left of them in the shallow river-bottoms or the rugged, windswept mountains. Nothing.

They bore down like an avenging juggernaut on Earth. Prepared to regain their lost heritage.

Prepared for anything...
...anything is what they found.

[EDITOR'S NOTE: Though "The Long Episode" concluded with the promise "Continued next month," Tim Richmond's FINGERPRINTS ON THE SKY lists no subsequent installments.]

Is the World Ready?
June 1953

Well, by now we've all had it. But good. Issue number three of Ziff-Davis's *Fantastic* is long ago out and by now the mind-numbing effects of seeing a banner headline reading: IN THIS ISSUE! MICKEY SPILLANE!! have worn off somewhat. But still the question remains, is the science fiction field ready for Mickey? Or for that matter is the science fiction world ready for Roy Huggins, Shirley Jackson, Billy Rose, or anyone of the other non-fantasy pros who have been introduced via that sterling publication to our ranks?

It may seem, at first glance, a moot point, but as Paul Ganley commented so caustically in a short article (somewhere or other, I can't remember where right now), "Sure Browne's trying to make converts... but from what: science fiction to the detective stories?" Which seems to be a perfectly justified assumption when you take a close look at what Howie boy has done. I've commented at length elsewhere on *Fantastic* itself, so there seems little point in rehashing that, but I'd like to go into this Spillane's recommendations for entrance into the highly specialized field of good and mature science fiction.

Mickey has spilled blood and guts to the tune of 15 million copies of his tripe sold (by the time this sees print that figure may be doubled, or even quadrupled for all we know) to eagerly upthrust and drooling muzzles of "The Common Man." At this point, the comment by John Mason Brown in *The Saturday Review of Literature* seems apropos: "Is our common man too common?" He has riddled more beautiful girls' bellies with more bullets than any sadist in the history of man with the possible exception of Mussolini who was sweetly addicted to this ginger-peachy pastime.

Mickey has gone from book to book with one theme in mind (variations stemming therefrom): get yourself a rough, stupid hero, let him beat the living bejezus out of all and sundry, let him wreak havoc with a suitable proportion of American womanhood's virginity, and finally wind up with a smash conclusion wherein there are corpses strewn about like crumbs for the foraging winter birdies.

In accord with the above procedure, Mickey has not let us down with his strikingly noxious opus entitled "The Veiled Woman." Browne must have paid a good ten cents a word for this...and I'd burn it for 10¢ per page. Or even better, I'll pay you to let me burn it. We find Spillane has cleverly combined a group of ideas completely unknown in science fiction (e.g., a lost race, a green woman, spies trying to wrest the secret from Our Boy, etc., etc., ad pass-the-bucket-ium) to make a soul-searing epic with such depths or social significance that THE DEMOLISHED MAN, THE LOVERS, and FINAL BLACKOUT all pale to insignificance before its masterful concepts.

If a total lowbrow such as myself may be permitted a summation of these transcendent abstractions, they might come out like this: "Always kick the other fellow when he's down, because he wants to swipe your wife from you, or because he ain't got as much dough as you, or because he's a damn' out-of-the-norm."

This is the closest approximation of what Spillane has brought to science fiction that I can muster. He has brought us the good-old barbarian custom of killing, the oldest profession in the world of obscene love-making, and some or the hoariest chestnuts of pre-antedeluvian science fiction that are scroungeable.

We owe a great deal to Messrs. Ziff, Davis, Browne, and Spillane.

They have opened new channels for the science fiction reader and writer. However, I'm afraid I'd be hesitant to tread those channels—toilet water may come streaming in at any moment.

Situation Scarlet
August 1953

MacIlhenny unstrapped himself and rubbed his chest slowly where the wide, leather acceleration strap had cut deeply. He squinted his eyes in the dim, half-gloom of the control room, and listened intently for a moment to the muffled throb of the reactor engines beneath his feet.

He ceased his unconscious rubbing, and strode toward the television screen set into the wall over the control console. A few moments' examination, the practiced twirl of a dial, and he reassured himself that the ship was functioning properly. He opened the pages of a metalloid book resting on a small shelf near the console inscribed, with a metal-tipped stylus, the words signifying the successful beginning of the second Venus expedition.

It was the year 2034. The Earth "beneath" them was still in turmoil. The planet Mars off to their "left" was in ferment also. And the bulk of the Luna spaceport, insignificantly dwindling in the lieu of their reactor blasts, too, knew the seeds of disquiet. Man was pursuing his eternal nature.

Yerman was unbuckling the heavy strap that held him to his bunk as MacIlhenny withdrew a plastic squeeze-bottle of hot coffee from a wall receptacle. "How's it look?" he mumbled through the after-blast thickness that acceleration had left in his mouth.

"So-so," answered MacIlhenny, around a mouthful of coffee. He squeezed another mouthful from the pliable container and gulped satisfyingly. Thoughts of other men before him doing the same brought sudden trepidation, clouding over the efficient relaxation that the smooth performance of the ship had encouraged.

The first Venus run.

Twenty-five point seventy-three million miles from Earth was a clouded mystery. A planet that had been called the sister to Earth. What lay beneath the clouds of supposed gasses? A ship had been sent out: an expensive and extensively supplied ship. That ship had erupted into a volcano of flame, three thousand miles out from Venus, erupting gouts of rent metal and exploded humanity into the deep of space.

Three years and thirty billions of dollars had fallen into the abyss of time before this second ship had boosted off from the Lunar base, bearing its three-man cargo, bearing its highly sensitized instruments, bearing the seeds of disquiet and the unquenchable inquisitiveness of man.

MacIlhenny snapped out of his reverie with a start, in time to see Frank Stock pulling on white sweat socks and a pair of the magnetized shoes that would prevent him from losing his weight, and, more likely, his lunch.

"How's she look?" Stock repeated the question Yerman had brought forth, a short time before. MacIlhenny felt a small mental grating at the repetition.

"Not so bad, I guess," he answered, swinging around. He walked out of the control room. Pulling himself off the floor by the hand bars near the sloping ceiling, he kicked backward lustily and shot down the winding corridor toward the off-duty salon.

Outside the ship, as clearly depicted by the television screen, an alien spaceship had coupled onto the titanium hull of the Venus-bound rocket. The very concept of an alien spaceship was bad enough, but to have it coupled on to *their* ship; Yerman was as near to frothing at the mouth as anyone MacIlhenny had ever seen. Stock was frozen to the console, his hands turning white under the force of his grip on the table. And MacIlhenny himself, a tall, blond man with shrewd green eyes, stared in disbelief at the sight of the softly glowing sphere that was attached to their bulk.

Stock opened his mouth to speak, but found that the words were dryly lodged against the roof of his mouth and that he had to wet his lips before the message would come forth. "At least this answers a helluva lot of questions," he said. "The Venus I blowing up, the weird patterns radar kept picking up with those bounced beams. The mystery of those clouds, and..."

"This doesn't answer a damned thing," interjected Yerman. "They could be from Wolf 359 for all we know. How the deuce you can take as big a set of unknowns as this and come up with what you think is a foolproof answer, is beyond me. Who the hell do you think you are, another Fermi?"

Anger flared momentarily in Stock's eyes. "Now wait just a minute, Phil, I wasn't..."

When the aliens entered the ship, they found the three Earthmen engaging in physical combat.

Stock picked himself up off the floor, nearly breaking contact with it and floating free in the ship when he saw them. There were three of them, tall, long-limbed, bipedal, with high foreheads and brilliant eyes. Their skin was a faintly off-color blue, as though it were turquoise superimposed just under the flesh, above a milky-white core.

They were imposing—all seven feet of each of them. And they bore no weapons.

Yerman, dripping crimson from a bruised lip, threw himself through the air toward his bunk, and came out with a service weapon that aimed itself almost mechanically at the foremost of the aliens. In the dead silence of the ship, the sibilant click as Phil Yerman brought the trigger back was like the deafening report of a million atomic bombs being set off at once. And the anti-climactic snarl as the automatic discharged its cargo toward the extraterrestrial called finis to the tension that had silently built up in the few moments since the aliens had come into the ship, while the three men had been pummeling each other.

The bullet sped unerring toward the chest of the alien, entered, was absorbed, the hole melted upon itself, and a moment later the alien withdrew from a previously non-existent bulge in the palm of his six-fingered hand, the assimilated bit of twisted lead.

The aliens turned to each other and for a moment or two clucked incomprehensibly to each other. Then they turned toward the three Earthmen with what was unquestionable fear, in the eyes; deep, consuming, petrifying fear. Dread. Loathing.

"They're afraid of us," screamed MacIlhenny. "Quick, do something to get them out of here!" He made a move toward the extraterrestrials, who cringed back, slinking toward the airlock from which they had recently emerged. Yerman began shrieking at the top of his voice, and Stock, who had been on his haunches ever since the strangers' entrance, kicked out with one leg at the retreating form of one of the blue-skinned fellows.

Clucking frantically, the three aliens turned and broke for the airlock, racing madly to escape some unseen terror. They were, quite obviously, frightened to the point of madness.

The airlock hissed behind them, and the Earthmen could hear the scurry of feet through the airtight coupling joining them to the alien sphere. They heard, faintly, at the other end, the hissing of air as the alien ship broke the couple, and through the medium of their television, they watched the softly glowing sphere barrel away from them at some incalculable speed. It disappeared rapidly into the star-bespecked fastness.

Surprise Package
October 1953

Semenole brought the bird down amidst a cloud of pale magenta sand
that billowed and flitted in all directions, radiating out in a monstrous
volatile cloud from the center, in which a spear of bright red flame
danced down from the blazing tube of the ship. Carventon buckled the
suit around himself as the last snapping shudder of the tubes' cooling
passed through the bulk of the machine, and lifted the helmet onto his
close-cropped auburn head. He stared momentarily at Semenole with a
bleak, bewildered stare; and then undogged the port, an auto-rifle held
much too tensely in his perspiring arms.

He itched under the suit, but he was damned if he'd scratch.

This was Earth?

This was the world that they had traveled 120 light-years from the
reassuring warmth of Spiga to see? This was what they must report to
the ancestors of those first fleeting Earthmen? To the flourishing races
on the planets surrounding Spiga they must carry a tale of Terra that
was dead and no more? Their ancestral home. So *this* was Earth.

(Something rustled in a burrow.)

Semenole joined Carventon on the desert. This, according to the
graphs, yellowed and falling to shards even in their lifetime-plastic
bindings, was the site of a place that the maps listed as New York.
According to the legend, this was supposedly the residence of millions
of people. But for all the distance they could see, to the very edges of
their vision, there was nothing but dead, red sand, sifting in over the
dwarfed and runted saw-grasses that heroically stuck their sickly gray
bodies up through the clinging quagmire of crimson particle.

Carventon shuddered uncontrollably. He pressed a button on the
console on his chest-box and a small feeder-arm came up from the
nearly skin-tight suit and inserted a cigarette between his dry lips. He
puffed it alight, and as the specially treated tobacco with their coated
inflammants took fire, the air purifyers in the helmet immediately
whisked the smoke out through the membrane at the end of the
multiple baffles in the excrete tube.

(Something sensed movement and started out into the light.)

They scuffed through the desert, away from the ship, which stood pointing up behind them like an accusing finger to the evening sky, the sun sinking into the now-ochre desert. A dead red orb with no appreciable aurora and an air of unhealthy, diseased existence. It threw monstrous, distorted shadows from them that spread out across the land before them like misshapen monoliths, transposed from some leprosied dream.

They topped a rise and stared down an embankment to a wall, rising out of the sand, weeds grown up about its bulk. Weathered and grayed like some ancient cadaver it posed there, a drunkenly tilted chunk of rock with no visible support to keep its fantastically tilted bulk aloft.

Semenole gawked for a moment and then yelled, the sound coming strained and unnatural through Carventon's speaker. With silent accord they pounded ankle-deep in the shifting sands down the shallow hill to the wall. The first sign of life and intelligence since they'd landed. Soft blubbering sounds came from Semenole as they neared it and he could detect inscriptions on the bare face of the stone wall. Semenole, the impressionable. He who had slaved and worked for ten years to get chosen from among all the entrees in the selections for who would go back to Earth.

Thirty generations was a long time to be away from one's ancestral home, and Semenole was one son of a son of a son who longed with a star-fire in his belly for the old home.

(Something emerged into the light and saw what had awakened him. Something called its brothers. They arrived and saw.)

Carventon puffed contentedly on his cigarette while Semenole pawed a rock with gloved fingers. Semenole was panting as he uncovered it. Perspiration formed on his helmet and was snatched away in mid-crystallization by the suit controls. Suddenly, he sank to his knees and began to whimper. Carventon watched, half-amazed, half-understanding as his partner of thirty months' journey weeped away the homesickness of thirty generations.

Semenole stood up and wiped his hand ridiculously across his helmeted eyes, realized he was crying and smiled nervously. He waved his hand toward Carventon and nodded him over to the wall where he read:

NEW O K PUBL C LI   ARY HOUR 9:   o 5:30
ADMIS   REE

They walked back through the blue darkening and talked of their dead home. Of the piece of rock beneath Semenole's arm that was the only indication that this *was* home.

They talked of what stages the Earth must have gone through before it died. Of the wars it had seen. Of the conquerors that beset it.

(The Conquerors mounted the steps to the ship and sighed the port shut after them. They proceeded calmly to the controls and prepared to take off. They noted the automatic settings dialed for the far colonies on Spiga's many planets. Revived action again after all these centuries...)

Semenole dropped the stone and yanked out his blaster; Carventon raised the auto-rifle his partner had carried before the weight of the rock had displaced it.

The Conquerors spread out in front of them in a sickening gray horde, tumbling back upon stomach over each other as they watched the first meal of centuries before them. The two children of mankind long-lost shook and retched with revulsion at the rows upon rows upon gatherings of them. Their suit purifiers were hard pressed to clean up the gorge.

Carventon and Semenole backed down toward the wall.

(The last thing the Conquerors saw as their ship, carrying them to the new feeding-ground, rose on a thin pillar of crimson, was the sight of the two bipeds backed against the wall, the torrent of rats sweeping in on them as they fired, blindly, helplessly...uselessly.)

The Pot o' Gold
January 1954

What hath I done? Little did I know when I printed "Farewell to Fandom" that it would be a bombshell.
KENT COREY

Ya'know, in this article, I agree with everything Ellison says, so he's not slurring me, or Elsberry. From now on, I'll never put any sort of editors [sic] notcs in any articles appearing in *Alice*. I'm sorry if I've hurt Uncle Harls [sic] feelings.
KENT COREY

AUTHOR'S NOTE: In *À La Space* #5 Richard Elsberry wrote an article called "Farewell to Fandom." Inserted therein were numerous and highly insulting comments by editor Kent Corey. Elsberry is a fellow whose opinions are more to [be] valued than most people's in fandom, and the insertion of Corey's remarks can be construed as nothing more than a flippant antagonism. There are no editor's notes in this article as I type it; if there are when it sees print, you will know that Corey is again being flippant and prostituting the work of his writers by inclusion of his own personal opinions. HE

[EDITOR'S NOTE: An editor's note by *À La Space* co-editor Lynn Hickman followed.]

There are many people in the fan world that I like. But there are few I respect. Respect is a commodity hard to come by, and one that entails a basic understanding and appreciation of the recipient. I happen to not only like Rich Elsberry. I happen to respect him.

Richard Elsberry is one of the few clear heads in fandom. He is one of a species that numbers less than twenty-five. He knows where he is going and he knows how to get there. Rich has said he is leaving fandom—and so it is. He will.

However, there is a side to the discussion that cannot be first glimpsed if just Rich's article is perused. This is definitely *not* a rebuttal of Richard's article or a condemnation, for what he says is as true for him as this article is true for me. It is the equivalent of saying: "Razor blades are better than lizard-skin traveling cases." There are two diversified personalities involved in this discussion, and probably more, and hence no solution can apply to all, of the temperaments involved.

Fandom to me is a "something" more than what Rich paints it. Certainly my basic reason for entrance into fandom was egoboo, but it was not that when I first came in, nor is it the sole motivating source now, and in years it will become increasingly important or—as I strongly suspect—of less immediate importance in my personal scheme of things.

Fandom was, originally, a source of companionship, with people who understood what I was thinking, what I was feeling, *why* I was feeling it, and could provide a certain complementary-ness to my emotions.

When I discovered the other unlimited vistas fandom unveiled, I was, at first, staggered and for a short time wallowed. Some fans never come out of that wallowing stage. These are the worshipful "neofans"; odious forms of stf-ists that bear an umbilical resemblance to spineless slugs. Some come out of that stage and recognize fandom as a gigantic chess board whereon you can become either a pawn, or one of the proportionally important players. Some, like Elsberry, Lee Hoffman, Redd Boggs, Dean Grennell, and their calibre, become bishops, knights, Queens, and...Kings of the game.

They get that way because they realize and utilize the potentialities of "the Game." I've realized a modicum of the possibilities of fandom and because of this, the rewards (along with the tithes and contretemps) have been great. There are times when I say to myself, "Christ, Ellison, throw in the sponge. You've gotten your egoboo. You're pretty much on top. You've done all you wanted to do in fandom. Check out while you're on the crest."

But then I take a look around and I see that during this jaunt in fandom I've picked up a fantastically wide background in magazine publishing, the inside of mimeography, the style of my own personal writing, hundreds of friends, opinions on every subject from Daschunds to Deep Space, my own magazine with my own name on the masthead, and a familiarity and awareness of the world about me that *never* could have come from my original circle of acclimation, why then I boggle a bit, swallow my Adam's apple and say to myself, "Hell, Ellison, look what you've done in just *this* long. Think what fandom and science fiction hold for you if you plow on and start out in fresh directions. Fandom is something special.

I'm not getting maudlin, because that isn't my nature. Nor am I heaving platitudes about like confetti. Fandom can afford, for the person willing to work his guts out, an outlet and a sponge to sop up his efforts like no other organizations or groups I've run across. You can have your Masons and your WCTU, but when it comes right down to sparkling, scintillating, fascinating, diversified, and original paths down which you can canter—lad, fandom is IT.

Sure Rich. I like Steinbeck, Capote, Ellison, and Hemmingway. But I like Heinlein, Bester, Budrys, Hubbard, and Leiber, too. I happen to like them for two different reasons. Steinbeck and his contemporaries feed me realism in raw, dirty chunks—and I gobble it up. But that's around me all the time. I read those lads because I wanted a different perspective of the world outside my apartment house. I read Heinlein and the rest of the sci-fic boys because I want to see what I've got to live for. I hate like hell having a bunch of pessimistic paranoids squawking in my right ear that the world is going to hell and gone in a dixie cup. I like to have Asimov tell me that there's a star cluster "out yonder" where Hari and his psych corps are whipping up a storm.

Face it brother, the world's not a particularly nice place, and aside from the catch-all phrase of "escape literature" that manages to stick to stf, I like to figure that if I'm going to die, it's better in a Nova (for *this* is the "year of the jackpot") than in some sludge filled bunker in Korea, or Ethiopia, or Transylvania, or where ever they decide to start shooting next.

Fandom *is* a way of life. It's a way of life founded, basically, on radicalism and unconventionalism. This is why I like it. Sure you can run up against your scum in fandom. You run up against it in your local movie theatre and on the subway too. That doesn't mean the whole system is wrong. Science fiction is a literature (that's right, I said a *literature*) that has unlimited possibilities, and a form like that HAD to spew forth fandom.

Being a fan is another way of saying, "I'm a cast-off. I can't get along with my herd." But, hell, as I like to say it, 89% of all advancement was made by misfits, and if a bunch of runny-nosed little fans can whip out a loosely knit organization like fandom with its own APAs, myriad magazines (regardless of the overall quality of same), yearly conventions where the pros feel it sufficiently worth their time to attend, and a cross-continental communications network that is so fantastic that you can know something that happened in South Dakota two [days] previously, it's well worth the keeping-up!

I hate adages, but there's one inescapable one that I'd like to reel off here to summarize. "You only get out of something what you put into it." There are breakdowns in that system, sure. Like Rich for instance. Rich has given a helluva lot to the field; his articles are among the best written in the ranks, and yet he didn't get his full measure out of fandom. That, I suspect, was in Rich, and not the fault of fandom as a whole.

Anyone can get screwed if they run up against the wrong customers on their entrance into fandom, and the trick is to get hooked up and affiliated and dealing with the right guys. FANDOM IS A HUGE POT OF

BRIGHT SHINY GOLD. If you happen to haul out a coin or iron pyrites, gentle reader, that, as they saying goes, is where you fell down.

My Gun Is Rusty
by Harlan "Blood&Guts" Ellison
January 1954

She stood in front of me, her lips parted, her eyes speaking a message of indescribable pleasure. Latonia was the most beautiful woman I had ever laid eyes upon. But she was bad, bad all the way clear through. Rancid.

She stood in front of me, swaying; she was wearing a tight pencil skirt with a built-in vacillation. Typical addict, I thought to myself.

I had tracked Latonia and her crew all the way from the slums of New York to this little Ohio resort town, and now I was so close to the answer, so close to the truth, that I wasn't going to let this enticing, beautiful, sexy wench throw me off the scent. At least not very much.

I remembered how it had all started, back on that cold winter day when I saw Alphonse, the most loyal beagle in the world, run over by a hopped-up Tootsie addict. I swore then that I'd get the creeps that were smuggling the Rolls in from Tahiti and Mexico.

When the head of the FBI called me in after I'd messed up a couple of petty Roll-runners in New York, I was mad. And when Spike Sledge gets mad, the whole underworld feels the tremor.

I sat opposite him, a butt dangling from my quivering lips, and my feet on his desk. "Whaddaya want, J. E.?" I spat. He shook noticeably. I had wetted his tie.

"How would you like to work with us on the Tootsie Roll menace, Sledge?" he asked.

I considered for a moment, snubbed my butt and cracked a new deck of Luckies. "Do I have my own way with this caper?"

He nodded.

And so I had gone looking for the low scum that were corrupting our school children, throwing small merchants out of business, ruining people's teeth, causing diabetes.

Latonia crooned huskily at me and I snapped my thoughts back into focus. She was unzipping her fur parka. I goggled.

The thoughts came unbidden into my mind. The picture of the cheap Club Charbere with its hazed-over smokiness and its frowzy patrons appeared in my head, reminding me of the chase that narrowed down till I had the low scum in the very grasp of my itchy gun-hand. I remembered walking into that dive and the stares of the inhabitants as they saw who I was. I heard the low hum go around the room that said, "Look out, here comes Sledge, he's looking for some low scum again and we of the underworld will soon feel the tremor!" I sidled unconcernedly over to the bar and pushed my snap-brim back on my head: "Gin-and-yogurt," I said out of the side of my mouth, throwing a fin on the liquor-stained mahogany.

I heard a laugh behind me.

I turned slowly, a pulse beating out "Night and Day" in my forehead. I could smell a fight a block away and getting nearer.

Standing behind me, a suspicious bulge under his dirty suede jacket, was Lew Leech, a known passer of Rolls. He was drunker than a skunk and the tell-tale dilation of his nostrils told me he was on a Roll binge to boot. "Something funny, Leech?" I rasped.

"Yeah, Shamus," he gurgled, the smell of cheap muscatel blanketing me, "you!" He went for his rod.

I had mine out before he could unzip the jacket, reach in, unbutton the holster flap, snap off the safety, whip the gun out, and fire. I clipped him along the jawbone with the barrel of the Smith and Wesson and felt the satisfying crunch of his dental plate crumbling beneath the impact. He staggered back, blood and teeth crimsoning in my bucks. "Lousy snooper," he rasped, sinking to the butt-strewn floor. "Now you'll never know that I was going to meet the head of the Roll pushing Ring in two days at a hotel in Columbus. You'll whistle for the info." I kicked him once in the gut and he doubled over. With a well-aimed blow I stuck my fingers in his eyes and he peeled over onto the floor.

"Your gin-and-yogurt," said the bartender quietly.

So here I was now, with the head of the Tootsie Roll ring moving toward me, her sinuous hips writhing out a message in semaphore that I could read all the way across the room, where I sat in the stuffed chair, my .45 pointed at her belly. "Sledge," she whispered, "I've come—"

I didn't giver her the chance.

I kicked the coffee table over on her and jumped up and down on it a few times for good measure. She got up and slowly began to unzip her form-fitting asbestos fire suit. She wanted to be mine. I couldn't stand it any longer. I aimed the Smith and Wesson carefully and shut my eyes. I heard a squeal from her and then the whole room blew up in my ears as the gun went off.

I had misaimed and there was a hole under her right armpit that was made by a bullet that went in clean and came out like a flying saucer, leaving a hole big enough to put my fist through. Blood and cartilage spattered the bookcase behind her. It was sickening. I can't stand the sight of blood.

Slowly she sank to one shapely knee, the cloth of her toga dripping crimson all over the deep pile rug. "Spike," she whispered through torn lips, "I—I—"

"Yeah," I screamed at her, "I know! We coulda had the world and each other! Well, I never wanted the world! All I wanted was to track the low scum that killed my dog! And it had to be you! It's rough, but I loved you and you were ran—er, rotten, through to the core! But I got the head of the Tootsie Roll ring!" I was bawling like a baby.

"Head, shmed," she gasped, her last breath rasping out wheezily as she died, "I came here to repair the television set!"

The Attack on
Alcidi El Boal
BEAU GESTE Revisited

by that sterling author
(sound of trumpet, horn, dulcimer, lyre,
etc.) Sheik Harlan Ben Ellison
March 1954

A staccato burst of light machine gun fire came through the window, shattering it into a tinkling mass. "Migawd, no," I screamed, clutching the bedclothes to my chin, "it's the militia come to drag me off to ROTC!"

I whimpered as I heard the tromp-tromp-tromp of their hobnailed boots in the courtyard outside. Then they shoved past old decrepit Mrs. Murtz, the landlady, and stormed up the stairs. There were twelve of them, all wearing the ill-fitting garb of the famed, yet dreaded, Desert Legion.

"You are ze one 'oo as mizzed five straight weeks of eight o'clock drill, non?" inquired a bearded giant with dark, glinting gray eyes.

"No, no!" I squawked, bulging my eyes and trying to assume an epileptic look, "I'm ill unto death (kaff-kaff!); I've been over to the Health Center (kaff-kaff!) and they told me I have acute Tyrannasaurus, can't march a step—you know how (kaff-kaff!) things are." I motioned feebly.

They grabbed me up by the legs and dragged me off, kicking and screaming, "Good Lord! It's twelve above out there, at least let me put something on over these shorts and T-shirt! I'll freeze!" But they relented not. I was borne off, on the upraised arms of the twelve heartless MSIVs.

When we arrived at the huge white stucco garrison at Alcidi El Boal, I was frozen stiff-legged and blue in a position of rigid erectness, like a ham shank left too long in Gus's icebox.

They dragged me before the Prefect, a cold, hard, calculating devil by the name of LeBanteau. The Prefect had dark, glinting black eyes and a scar running across the bridge of his nose, down into his collar and emerging again from his sleeve. Man, what a knife fight *that* must have been.

He stared at me with his dark, glinting, green eyes and flipped a dirty Kleenex at me in deprecation: "Zo," he said, "you 'ave been mizzing drill ze last five weez, n'avez-vous pas?" I shook my head negatively. "Ah-ha," he crowed, leaping to the top of his filing cabinet, upsetting a bowl of chickenfat cooling there, "he admits it! Zis iz listed in ze Manual under section 42, part N, paragraph Q-6, sub-heading 4, number 337.925.8 as 'Insubordination unfitting the demeanor of a recruit—CUTTING' Throw him in the Bastlead." The Bastile had rusted away some time ago.

He threw me one last look with his dark, glinting blue eyes and turned toward the window, nodding to the guards to carry me off. At that moment a dum-dum bullet came exploding through the window plowing into the Prefect and leaving a hole as big as a flying saucer that you could have stuck your fist into. "Sledge, Spike Sledge," he gasped, as he sank to the linoleum, "I'm a-goin', pard, but ah want yuh ta get the dirty bushwacker thet cashed in muh chips, pard!" He expired noisily.

A frenzied guard came rushing in, screaming, "The Boors, the Boors, they're attacking the Fort. *C'est la vie!*"

I shot him for inciting a riot and commanded the guards to unthaw my legs as I donned a pair of the late Prefect's pants. Now my only problem was the defense of Alcidi El Boal against the ravages of the marauding desert hordes of the Boor leader, Sheik Aly Ben Epstein. Hmmmm, I thought, we must have some special trick to be able to outwit the ravages of the marauding desert hordes of Sheik Aly Ben Epstein. Then it hit me!

A brick tossed through the window with a note tied on it.

I picked it up and tore the note free from the string. It was written in blood on papyrus in a rare cuneiform hieroglyphic, and was unsigned. Right off I sensed something odd about this letter. Most of my mail was signed.

I deciphered the message and read the words that struck cold notes in my heart. It said that my subscription to *Better Homes and Deserts* had run out. A crushing blow.

But I straightened by back, donned my fez, and commanded the soldiers to take up their arms and place themselves all along the wall of the fort, facing in all directions, ready to ward off the ravages of the marauding desert hordes of the Boor Leader, Sheik Aly Ben Epstein. The last picture of the Prefect's dark, glinting orange eyes stirred in my mind as I watched the desert for the attack.

Then I heard it: the thrum-dum-dum of a thousand horses' hoofs cascading across the heat-stifling wastelands of the desert. The Sheik was a-comin'! No shrimp boats, just the Sheik. I glanced at my watch. High noon!

The sound rolled over us like a monstrous tidal wave, driving terror, fear and apprehension into my stomach. The pain of them was horrible. They ached and throbbed. And no Pepto-Bismol handy. What a situation! I heard a shot off to my right and turned just in time to see one of my men, a faithful desert legionnaire by the name of Newford Carr, topple to the dust of the courtyard, a Polka-dotted Boor spear sticking from his belly. It was a kind of Boor Belly Polka.

The sounds of fighting raged all about me as the picture of the swarthy, dark, glinting-eyed Boors swam before my perspiring face. Sweat ran down my back in raging torrents. I nearly drowned. I fired at random into the horde. But Random was a helluva thin man and being very agile escaped harm. He shook his fist at me, though, and swore to return later.

The other Boors came on again, brandishing old Commerce College cards, with which they tried to brain my men. I lifted an automatic rifle off a corpse, thumbed it onto automatic fire and braced it against my shoulder. With a fervent prayer to the sky I squeezed the trigger. The rifle leaped in my hands and liquid fire spurted from the mouth of the weapon. The Boors scattered like a 4:00 on Friday.

Unfortunately, their strength was far superior to ours and after regrouping, they charged once more. Over the hum and buzz of their horses and their voices I could hear a steam calliope playing the Boor national anthem—"Do Not *Desert* Me Oh My Dromedary"—as the sound of native screams broke on my ears.

Suddenly I knew what rouse would outwit the fanatical ravaging marauding hordes of the Boor leader, Sheik Aly Ben Epstein. With a cry to the men, I gathered them in the courtyard and told them to make haste to follow my instructions.

When they perceived what I had in mind they clapped me on the back vigorously. One legionnaire even started the cheer, "Vive la Sledge. Vive la—" I shot him for inciting a riot. Knew I should have learned French.

The men followed my directions and, alone, I waited, golden sun beating down upon the late Prefect's dirty pants and myself in my scuddy T-shirt and Desert Legion cap. Then I heard it coming closer and closer.

The super-chief. It buzzed through the wall of the garrison and tore out the other side. Damned railroadmen: don't give a damn *where* they lay their track! But even that did not deter me. I stood steadfast and sturdy, waiting for the barbarians to come and kill me.

Of a sudden they burst through the break in the wall, firing at random about the courtyard. But Random, having switched sides, was leaping about the courtyard agilely, causing the natives much consternation. Even though they were busy with him, the Boors grabbed me and I was dragged before their leader, a tall, high-browed, crafty-looking man with dark, glinting red eyes. *This* was the Sheik Aly Ben Epstein.

"Zo," he spat, "you are ze indomitable Spike Sledge, scourge of ze desert." I nodded. He spat. I nodded. He spat. This time he got me. I wiped the spat off my forehead and clenched my fists. I watched him in silence. It was a thin, whispy silence that had settled about my legs while I stood there.

"Where are ze rest of your men," the words came out clipped.

"What men?" I replied, playing it cool.

"Infidel, clod, scum, pig's left shoelace, freshman, son of a son of a too bad CENSORED!" He was enraged. He leaped about, rasing large clouds of dust.

I winced. "Please," I asked him, "would you mind not rising so much dust. Hurts my allergy. Makes me sneeze." I sneezed for him. It was a dandy sneeze.

The Boor leader was enraged even more: "Take him away. Show him the death of a thousand tortures, while we try to find the rest of his men." They carried me away. But just as I lost sight of him, I saw the Sheik sitting on the ground, pouting, and I heard him say, "Nasty mans, hid all his men—took all my fun away. No tortures, no blood-lettings; that nasty mans!"

The natives took me to the desert and dug a hole, put me in it with my arms tied behind my back, and filled the hole back up again till only my head was above the sand. Then they commenced the most ghastly of tortures known to man. They fed me Tavern food for three hours.

But even as the lights dimmed and I knew I was heading for that Big ROTC Drill Session in the Sky, I rejoiced, for I knew the Sheik would never find my men.

You see, I had disguised them as packages of chicken noodle soup. Vive la Mrs. Grass!

Seven on 53rd
Spring 1954

AUTHOR'S INTRODUCTION: This is trite. And it isn't very original. Nor does it have any great stature or social significance. In all analyses, it stands forth as a rather poor experiment into violence. I enjoyed writing it immensely. It wrote itself in fifteen minutes and not one word of correction has been done on it. To my mind it has a great feeling of nail-hardness. Opinions are desirable, in all their sound and fury. But that won't change it—I like "Seven on 53rd" very much. Perhaps, well, perhaps it happened to a very close friend of mine, a guy I shave every morning.

There is an air about seven o'clock. You can feel it in the surge and beat of the crowd. You squint down the street, into East 53rd, and you feel the press and ebb of the people as they go about their seven-ish ways.

Seven o'clock.

Scuff of shoes against dirty milk-container on the sidewalk, and it skitters into the gutter. Oil slick in the street reflects back the colors of the bar across the way. It never used to be there. Some little whop had his shoe repair shop there, as you recall. A new bar; a new experience.

You cross the street and the rasp of tires slipping on the wetness of the blacktop startles you and quickly your head snaps up to see a car just skidding to a stop. Close. But then everything's close. Living—and dying. And even paying taxes, if you want to get cute about it.

The bar's name wiggles across the top of the two-storey structure, a multi-colored snake thing. You can't even tell what it says. Might be the "Seven O'Clock Club" or "Kit Kat's Korner" or "Sammy's" or any one of a thousand names, but they all smell bad, and in the same way. The stink of cheap liquor and cheaper people.

There is a small brass railing in front, and a flight of stairs that lead downward into a depth that promises nothing but a jigger of VO and a leer at a sodden barfly. Sound of laughter in your head. Soft.

The door swings open and you swagger in.

There are people, of course.

They all fit into molds. You've seen the same faces in a numberless eternity of bars, but they never change. Not in the least. They're all big and small, dirty or clean, peroxide and natural. They all have the feeling of life about them. It's funny you muse, you can feel *life* more clearly in a bar than anywhere else in the world. Why is that?

You cross over to the bar itself and lean your frayed leather-jacketed elbows on the liquory mahogany. A shrunken dwarf of a man with the bald skin of his head being pulled tight across his forehead till it has a blue shine to it comes from nowhere and you automatically rattle off your brand. His watered-down blue eyes disappear and then you look around. Deep and nothing, like the belly of a porpoise. Dark. Smoke.

In the back, in a booth, a truck driver's loving up a waitress who squeals falsetto as he tickles her. You turn your face away in disgust. Down the bar your glance ranges and you type them one after another. They aren't people—they're types:

There's a barfly (he's got a two-day growth on him, he smells from having slept in a doorway with pages from the *Post* under his thin jacket, his fingernails are coal-dust black, and he stares deep into his glass seeing pictures of things that never can be); there's a B-girl (her skirt is too tight, the seam is splitting, her sweater's too tight, it'll get her an extra drink or two, she wets the tip of her cigarette); there's a guy whose wife hates his guts and stupid smile (he sweats too much, the babe on his arm is trying to get away from the smell, she's giving that sailor the eye and the sweater doesn't like it. His hands are cold and his breath comes fast. He doesn't want her to leave him because then he'll have to go home to the bitch); there's the sailor out on leave (he wants to get drunk and wind up with a body in bed, that's all).

Types.

And what are you?

What type are you?

You look at yourself in the bar mirror, with the pyramids of streaky glasses in the way, and you see a guy whose mind is blank. You aren't thinking. At least not about anything worth thinking about. Just the types, that's all. And *their* story is written in their dead eyes.

Your drink comes and you flip a half-dollar onto the counter, nodding to the dwarf in the dirty apron. You pick up the drink and sniff the booze. Lousy crap! There's a ring on the bar and you put the wet bottom of the jigger down on it twice more and make the sign of that beer commercial. You still aren't thinking.

Oh, hell!

You pick up your glass again and grip it tightly in your right hand feeling the curved top of the jigger, serrated, like a flower petal. With a strength from nowhere you heft it in your hand, spilling some of the amber fluid on your palm, and toss the goddam thing all the way across the room. It smashes with a tinkling shatter on the wall and sprays the truck driver with bourbon.

You aren't thinking.

He comes up out of the booth, a big guy, leaving the rumpled waitress pouting, and comes at you with a snarl that's strictly from the jungle. He's got a beer bottle in his hand and he's got it leveled like a street-fighter would use it. You stick out your foot and catch him in the groin with your knee. He bellows like a poled cow and you swing with all the strength in your arm. He walks straight into it and you feel the sickening crunch of bone and cartilage under your knuckles.

The guy bellows again and blood starts to spurt from his nose.

Jesus! You think, I'm no hoodlum, what the hell am I fighting in here for? You drop to your knees and grab the guy by the shoulders, crying into his face and telling him over and over that you didn't mean it, that you're sorry as all hell. The guy looks bewildered. He doesn't know whether to split your head open for ruining his nose or start crying with you because you're so pathetic looking.

You drag the bulk of your wallet out of your hip pocket and draw out a wrinkled five spot. You slip it into his hand, now covered with his own blood, and leg up that flight of stairs out onto the street above.

The whip of the fresh air hits your nostrils and you breathe deep and try to cleanse your mind along with your chest. And somewhere back in a hollow of your mind, that laughing. Clear. Soft.

Then you start to think?

Where did you get the leather jacket from? Where did you get the money from? Where the hell are you? How the hell did you get where you are, and above all, WHO ARE YOU?

There's a flapping something caught in a wire fence at the back of your mind. Caught and flapping. It's a picture of a white man and fist and someone being shoved in a closet and a big joint with windows that never show lights and a ditch and walking and walking and walking.

You hear the high keening whine of a police car. You know it's a prowl car even before you see the beetle-like thing.

You break into a run and a beer can crunches flat under your foot as you slam into an alley and crouch down behind a garbage box loaded with old cardboard containers. The flash of lights reveals and reflects off the bare brick of the alley wall and the puddles or urine from a trash carrier's horse, and then disappears as you hear the solid thunk of a cop car's door slamming. They're looking for you, boy. You. You!

How the hell did you get into this?

Then there's a period of gray running. Nothing but milky grayness shot through with silver streaks of pain as you run. Flee!

Where are you fleeing to? Where are you running: where do you go?

Then you fall on your face and the droplets of mud splash up across the bridge of your nose and the thin line of scar on your cheek, and you sleep. Closed up in the soft cocoon of sleep you lay there, closed up to the world, and you don't even rise as the men with the white jackets screech up in their ambulance and slip the jacket with the leather thongs on you, imprisoning your arms across your chest.

You breathe deeply and slumber as they trundle you into the ambulance with its mud-spattered white sides. The ambulance that has the legend STATE ASYLUM FOR THE CRIMINALLY INSANE printed across it.

You'll sleep for a long time.

And in the back of your head, that laughing. Soft. Pitying.

The Game of Chance
Spring 1954

It was clearly a pinball machine. There were colored lights and poorly delineated drawings spotting a wormy board underneath, and he stood poised before it with a nickel in his hand. He took the worn coin firmly between his fingers and dropped it swish-click down the slot.

Machinery whirred and things began to snap into place as the game re-began itself for the short spurt ahead. He dropped his shoulders, hunched them and pushed the drive shaft on the raising mechanism forward with a passion. A small silver sphere popped up out of the hole and jounced to a rest at the end of the corridor. Twisting it but gently in his palm he drew the coiled spring-rod back—and let it snap. The ball sped out of the shaft, straight as a hairline, caromed with the bend of the back board, hit the metal deflector, and the Game began once again in an eternity of players and re-plays. The pattern set.

He stood there looking crestfallen. The multi-colored glass in front of him read 3 million (in big yellow), 200,000 (in only slightly smaller red), and down in the corner 90,000 (in very small orange). He was torn. Five balls and only 3, 2, 9! What a stinking machine. He slammed the cigarette-burned guard rail against the glass top and the machine clicked. He stared, wide-eyed. It read, in bold slanting green figures: TILT.

His time was up. He didn't have another nickel. The game was over.

Where Was I?
April 1954

Where was I when it landed? I remember distinctly lying down on my couch to read a fanzine (I've been trying to dredge up every facet of the thing but that one point, the name of the fnz, won't come through) and suddenly falling asleep. And the next thing I knew it was ten hours later and the thing had landed, talked to Mamie, and gone. Now if anyone should have talked with him (if it was a him) it most assuredly should have been me.

The way I get the story, about an hour after I fell asleep there was a monstrous humming and buzzing heard over the White House and this flying saucer lands on the Truman Portico. Even *I* would have scoffed at the ridiculousness and the sheer crass commercial movie tactics of the pilot in landing on the White House grounds. But that's the way the e. t. did it, so how the dickens can you doubt it? You can still see the circular cracks running around the Portico where the blamed thing settled its bulk.

As far as I can get them to tell me, the shiny, saucer-like vessel opened and out popped this little three-foot high "man" with green skin, three eyes, and a propeller beanie with a birdbath instead of the traditional rotors (those damned insurgents) on it. Right away all the guards at the White House start pumping slugs at the alien but he just waltzes away from them and they bounce off a resistor screen or something like that. Into the building he walks and demands in the most fluent of English to see someone that nobody there has ever heard of. He jumps up and down and keeps screamin' he wants to see this character, but the guards don't know what to do to quiet him.

Right about then Mamie comes down the stairs and she invites the green fellow into the drawing room for some tea and a chat. Well, it works out that he's from somewhere off beyond Orion and he just wanted to stop over on his way somewhere or other to see somebody on Earth. Well, Mamie gives him the old gazaboo about formalities, and he should come back over Labor Day etcetera.

So he goes back to the saucer, hops in and takes off. About a day later, fifteen F.B.I. men come and haul me out of the house, lug me to Washington, and set me up in front of Mamie and she tells me that they're going to hold me there till next Labor Day. I tell her that I gotta be in Philly but she just gives me the fisheye and says words to the effect of "Oh yeah?"

So here I gotta sit. I don't know if he's coming, but Labor Day ain't as far off as I thought. Ya know, I always thought my fanzine had a wide circulation, overseas and all, but this is the first time I've ever had a reader come from Orion to see me.

Saboteur Symbiote
September 1954

Around the base of the rocket ship the ant-sized figures of men in working clothes scurried, back and forth, back and forth, racing madly with time. With time that had decreed the winner of the War to be the first country on the Moon. The scene with its atmosphere of fantastic unreality, huge banks of Klieg lights—and powerful beams of fluorescence—was taking place somewhere in the heart of New Mexico. Everyone on the project was well aware of the fact that somewhere—somewhere—perhaps on the frozen steppes of some faraway land, another rocket was being built.

A race with time.

Up the side of the metal cylinder, the elevator whirring quietly, went a mechanic with a soldering iron. A nondescript mechanic, like anyone of the other three hundred mechanics signed on for Project Pumice.

Up the side of the shining hulk till he came to an "I" beam that protruded off from the side of the scaffolding, housing a multi-tangled webbing of unsoldered wires. He stepped lightly off the elevator onto the scaffolding and plugging the soldering iron into the socket provided, began to join the loose connections.

...no one noticed the thin wisp of volatile protoplasm seep out of nowhere and skitter for an instant to and fro in normal space before plunging toward one of the workmen. He stooped to retrieve a dropped implement and the nearly invisible bit of matter shot over his head and toward the bulk of the spaceship. It struck it with no effect and went sliding up the ship till it caromed off the scaffolding upon which stood the mechanic with his soldering iron. The protoplasmic visitor rushed pell mell for the soldering iron and without a trace of where it had gone, slid noiselessly inside. The mechanic carried on his duties.

The iron quivered, broke out of the man's grip, tore loose from the socket, bounced off the metal bulkhead—and smashed the mechanic's head into a queerly sodden ball of blood-bedecked jelly.

They sat about the table, concern lining their faces, tension evident in every movement of their perspiring bodies. Silence pervaded and surrounded the room. Someone began nervously ticking a pencil against his teeth and the others looked askance at him until he sensed their irritation and in confused embarrassment giggled like a child caught in some pointless endeavor.

"Well, there's a spy among us—what do we do about it?" inquired Numering. "We thought we'd screened them all...but one seems to have gotten past. What do we do? I can't head up Communications and handle Screening and Public Relations too." Petulance forced his lower lip out.

One of the men in uniform pulled a black cigar from his pocket and began chewing distractedly on its end. Finally he answered, "We have to get this ship up in two weeks. I know it—you know it—and the saboteur knows it. He also knows that we can't do another screening because we'd fall behind schedule more than we are now. I don't know what's going to happen. 500 persons is a nice round figure, but a helluva lot to start checking on.

Each of the men, at one time or another during the discussion, had followed the train of events mentally and seen what had occurred in its proper sequence. First, about two weeks previously, one of the scaffolding jockeys had somehow or other gotten his head bashed in: no satisfactory explanation. Second, the second scaffold on the north tier had given way and seventy men had plunged to either death or disfigurement; no satisfactory explanation. Third, one of the Klieg banks tore loose from the chain and crashed into the Analyzer shed, killing seven technicians and completely demolishing three computers, including the new EDVIAC II brought in from MIT. Four... Oh, it could go on for quite some time; a list of deaths and destruction that immediately discounted chance and brought out the word saboteur.

"I suggest we..."

...no one saw the almost invisible entity that shot through a wall of the council room, rebounded off the light fixture, and plunged into the head of a beefy army colonel.

"...know by what means just who had access to the Klieg elevators and also had a means of..."

Colonel Gorham stood up quietly—all heads swivelled to see what the interruption was for—and just as quietly he pulled out his service automatic and sent a bullet into the head of each of the men in the room, including himself.

Off somewhere beyond the Pleiades, far far from the sun Sol there revolves a small blue planet about an equally blue star. In the "cities" of that planet faint shapes weave back and forth and in one of the "buildings" of one of those cities is an agency devoted exclusively to tracing. For the "people" who infest this world have learned to know the limits of their abilities. They are fully aware of the damage to be inflicted by one of their number if such one should leave the mother planet.

These are beings of intelligence, worldly wise, farers of space for eons but consigned to one planet by their own decree. The "agency" had been inactive for more than fifty decades. But now...

Needless to say, the implications of one of their number leaving the planet and venturing forth into space were enough to bring back into service that departmental force. From the home planet spewed forth forty thousand agents, dispersed into all sectors and directions of the known universe. Tracing the burst pen-atoms' trail, they sought that one miscreant who dared to break the most important law of their existence.

One such agent, an entity named Fluour-kreff, while passing through the Centaurian worlds, detected a nearly worn-away trail left by the exploding pen-atoms. Flashing toward the trail he detected their direction and without a moment's thought released a reservoir of stored-up energy within him and sped toward one spiral cluster not far away. Into the cluster, plunging deeper, deeper, into the swarm until he pulled up short just outside the orbit of a green planet that revolved about a luminous yellow star. The trail was still fresh, the pen-atoms registering their broken components on his mental retinas.

Down toward the planet, many times the speed of light, shipping about the planet, surging forward as the trail led to a portion of the planet consisting mostly of desert. Out across the desert at a much slower speed till encountering a group of humanoids endeavoring to wreak some sort of havoc upon an insensitive piece of metal. Here the trail was still being made.

Here, it was, that the runaway had come.

Fluour-kreff entered the head of George Pemberly very quietly, mixing with his thoughts those of the host.

I am from another world.

"I am aware of that," thought George Pemberly.

Then you know why I am here.

"Yes."

Do you think you can help me locate the errant one?

"Not only do I think I can help you find him, I have already managed to trace the one you seek. He is now in the person of a man named Carthwright. A pilot."

Where is this Carthwright now?

"Come with me."

I have no choice.

"Nor have I."

Within the brain of George Pemberly, Fluour-kreff resided, thinking. The tremendous mentality of the being stunned the Earthman with its incalculable immensity. The thought, pure in logic and unhampered by useless prejudices, came through unsullied by false reasoning.

"You are quite an intellect," ventured George Pemberly.

The entity laughed lightly.

The being's thoughts mixed with those of the Earthman; each knew the other's most sublimated memories—yet heightened, with a subtle interflowing sense neither could define, that was something totally new—and immensely powerful.

"The one you seek must indeed be a genius to have escaped the circumstances to which it should have conformed. Such intelligence and power of wisdom is staggering."

This time the entity might have been considered to be roaring with laughter.

"There is Carthwright."

The entity looked out through the eyes of George Pemberly and saw a huge pit, lined with lead, and nestling in it a spaceship exactly like the one that domineered the scene save the fact that it was only twenty feet high.

"In that ship, which is a test model, is loaded a cache of atomic fuel which can explode at any time the proper mechanism is tripped. It was so constructed in the eventuality that a necessity for its being destroyed should arise. I saw Carthwright loading more warhead material in there this morning. At the time I didn't realize why he was doing it, but with all this talk about saboteurs, I strongly suspected him. Is that the one you seek? Can you tell?"

Yes, the pen-atom trail leads directly to that ship. What is the purpose of his loading the ship in that manner?

"He might try to crash-dive it back into the project. There's enough high explosive matter at critical mass in there to wipe most of New Mexico off the Earth. Why would he do something like that? A being of his obvious intelligence? What have we done to..."

Suddenly the ship began to tremble and a thread of flame seeped out from beneath it. The model of the monster ship clawed frantically at the air, rising on tiptoe till it shoved itself off. With a roar it sped off and up, up, up into the midday light, disappearing with each passing second.

Fluour-kreff massed his potential and with a wrench—slung the body of George Pemberly up into the noon sky in pursuit of Carthwright and his burden.

Carthwright turned and saw George Pemberly standing behind him. Neither spoke. But within their heads a turmoil was being begun. The two entities recognized each other and locked in the most primary force-of-arms of mentality. There ensued a climbing of the mental ladder, up and up and up to reaches of mental power unknown to the Earthman.

Suddenly, there was a snapping sound...

The entity within the mind of Carthwright slithered out from the eyes, from the nose, from the millions of pores of his face, and coalesced into a shining blob of protoplasm between George Pemberly and the suddenly ashen pilot.

We'll be getting back now. The entity named Fluour-kreff said.

George Pemberly answered, "It is a source of happiness to me that I have been able to help one such as you. In the future, however, it would seem advisable to keep a better hold on the great minds of your planet. Another such brilliant one as this might ruin the galaxy."

As the two entities slid out through the bulkhead, one in custody, the other the custodian, George Pemberly's brain received the last message from the volatile being:

You have ascertained the wrong solution, friend. This is not one of our great minds...this is an escaped imbecile.

Come Back, Little Birdbath...a tragedy

October 1954

ACT I: SCENE ONE
(*sounds of fruit hitting the stage*)

SCENE: *garbage pit just outside the city limits of Bratislava. Two filthy, unkempt, slovenly, fly-ridden, diseased members of the People's Government crouch over a small fire, toasting each other's feet. Popalov speaks:*

POPALOV: Hit's ha gud ting ve find dis garbage pit. Ve starve to det on old moldy borscht if not.

GUZBAVITCH: Da.

POPALOV: (*shivering*) Tell me, Comrade, you really ting dis People's Guvamint all is crocked up to beink?

GUZBAVITCH: Da.

POPALOV: All time "Da!" Is dot all you can say?

GUZBAVITCH: Da.

Popalov, enraged, hoists his Mauser rifle and draws a bead on Guzbavitch. It is a large red bead and with a howl the starving Popalov shoves it into the other's eye. Guzbavitch, annoyed by this boorish conduct, expires noisily and Popalov, exceedingly irritated by the trend the conversation has taken throws a fit of temper and in a pique eats Guzbavitch.

POPALOV: Urp.

The murderer, fearing among other things, for his life, decides to flee.

POPALOV: (*packing small bits of Guzbavitch in an old Ritsky Cracker box*) I will flee dis place of det. I vill strike oud on mine own for the vast vorld dot vaits beyond de horizon.

At this point the Author, sensing impromptu padding of the part, stalks onto the stage in the garb of a Russian Boris (the Kremlin version of a Bobby) and lays mightily on Popalov's head with a prop belaying pin from off stage.

POPALOV: Dammit, stop dat. It hurts!

BORIS: Get off dis stage, you creepsky.

POPALOV: (*planting foot in Author's groin*) Da, I leave for Camelsky, on the shore of da Carbolic River.

BORIS: Get oud! Ged oud!

POPALOV: I'd valk a mile for Camelsky. (*He exits left, bleeding from lacerations about the face and head, laughing wildly at his punsky.*)

AUTHOR: Dot creep. Ve ged oud Philadelphia, ve switch cast on dot slob. Ged Barrymore. (*He exits right, clutching himself awkwardly.*)

END SCENE ONE

ACT I: SCENE TWO

SCENE: *Garbage pit, three hours later. Nothing is doing. Orchestra leader plays a few bars of "June Is Busting Out All Over," notices no one is paying any attention, kicks cymbalist out of spite and gives the whole thing up as a bad deal.*

END SCENE TWO

ACT II: SCENE ONE

SCENE: *City of Camelsky. Popalov, seeking sanctuary, has been led to the home of Catanya Crowsbagle, a member of the underground. Popalov speaks:*

POPALOV: Dark down here, isn't it?

CATANYA: Vot you ekkspect, the Taj Mahal? Dis is the underground. In foct, is de most underground underground available. Ve so underground ve got trouble locating ourzelves sometimes.

POPALOV: Catanya, anyvone effer tell you, you are *gorjuss* hunk voman?

CATANYA: Da.

POPALOV: Now you stottink dot too! Alla time mit "Da! Da!" Shtop it!

CATANYA: Mine Dahlink, slow down. Stop grindink yoo gears! Cahme offer here lettink me soothe you fevered browsky.

POPALOV: Soothe me.

CATANYA: Sooth, soothe, soothe, soothe, soothe...

At this point, Author, in the rather mildewed garb of a transient candle-dipper, casting furtive glances to the League of Human Decency delegation in the front row, sees that Popalov and Catanya are going to make one helluva orgy of the whole thing and bursts in, dripping tallow.

CANDLE-MAKER: To arms, to arms! The Secret Police are comink!

POPALOV: Vat is dis! Geddoudda here!

CANDLE-MAKER: (*aside*) Wadya tryin' ta do, ya slob, get me banned?

POPALOV: (*drawing scimitar*) Bolshevist! (*He severs Author's head from shoulders.*)

END SCENE ONE

ACT II: SCENE TWO

Curtain goes up too soon, audience sees stage hands frantically mopping up profuse amounts of blood and gore, with OcellO sponges and squish-handle mops. Everyone looks sheepish. Stagehands look at each other, throw arms about each other's shoulders, crouch and begin doing Schottishe, singing lewd choruses from "Song of the Tartar Martyrs." Audience looks alarmed. Curtain descends in nick of time.

END SCENE TWO

ACT III: SCENE ONE

SCENE: *Courtyard just outside jail, as seen through Popalov's cell window. Gallows. Popalov mounts. He speaks. With faltering voice. No wonder; he had a rope looped around his esophagus.*

POPALOV: Vy I gott die? Vy me? I been goot boy all my life. I luff People's Guvamint. Only vun ting I effer done wrong. I kilt Guzavitch, Crowsbagle, unt old Candle-dipper vot was really Author in dizguize.

HANGMAN: Da.

POPALOV: Must you?

HANGMAN: Da.

POPALOV: (*enraged, but unable to scream because of rope*) I report you to House *Un*-Camelsky Activities Committee! I show all you noodnicks! Vot you tink bout dot? (*He gloats*)

HANGMAN: (*releasing trapdoor*) I pussnally dunt giff a damn. Dey takink me off dis job tomorrow anyhow.

POPALOV: (*with dying gasp*) Vot you gone be now?

HANGMAN: Author. Bye.

Curtain & Popalov fall simultaneously.

THE END

Vista
December 1954

The view from here is desolate.

Try staring out across the crazy-quilt that is my world. At the big blue and the small crystal white of the rock formations. At the lusterless water that burbles noncommitally through deserts of shifting green sands. At the huge pocks that show the idiocy of too much talent, not quite enough intelligence.

Oh God, whatever God watches this place, why did you let this happen? Why did you let my people learn the hate, and then to find the absolution of that hatred? My horns dip as I think of it, my tail beats the dull green sands to a mist, my cleft tongue whispers hoarsely.

No longer do my skies cry out with the agony of being ripped apart by a silver-winged horde of missiles. No longer does the air above the long, deep deserts whistle with the scream of explosive shells.

Now for the longest time, all has been silence...

There is no one else here. The view is brittle-metal cold and as desolate as only a world lost can be. Tears, starting not from eyes, but from ducts in my cheeks, course down my scaled flesh. Where are the spirits of my lost brothers? Even those have fled from this home they once knew so well.

They scattered through the spaces between worlds, overrunning, challenging, winning. They were a new and vibrant factor in the weave of the plans of fate. But they carried the germ of dissension.

Never fear, you other, hidden races of the skies. My people will never find your judiciously secreted homes far away. They are gone forever. The universe will spawn and spawn once again, but never the bright, blue flames that they were.

The view from here is merciless.

The sun has gone old and diseased. It burns down like a man in fever at a world as sick as he. Mountain tops sheared off as though a circular saw had eaten their heads away. Nothing moves. Nothing sighs. Nothing, even, in the immortal and unchanging pattern of everything, whimpers after its parent. Even the children are so long nothing that they seem a fantasy.

Oh God, whatever God is cruel enough to allow this, is not there some peoples four hundred sextillion miles off across the nebulæ, behind some fathomless pit in the charcoal of space, who were a fraction of a decimal point more deserving of extinction? Why *my* people?

My skin shifts from focus to focus as I remember them; with the smiling faces; the powdery hands giving and receiving some good, too.

The power of the atom is manifold.

I once walked on two legs, made love with two arms; saw, smelled, talked with a symmetrically arranged face. I was once a man.

I am distorted. I will never die; I am immortal. I am alone on this hell-pit that was once a green and brown and white and blue world.

You know this world.

Swamp Dust
December 1954

There wasn't an awful lot of use to it. We knew Mose was out there. We knew he was logged up somewhere out in that five mile strength of big stink and green nothing with his forehead sweated and his hand wrapped thick around the gun. The trouble was, *where* in the swamp was he, and how were we supposed to get him out.

We all met on the front porch of the Sheriff's office, with our squirrel-rifles or Lugers brought back from Anzio or Paris. Fred Shutt was there, wearing his big brown glasses. He was looking sick about the whole thing. But then, maybe he should have—you might think he was the cause of it all.

Mose Oliver had been a pretty silent type. We all knew he wasn't right up there, but we didn't see no call to be pestering him, so we just avoided him like. He'd walk along the dirt street past Naylor's General Store, wearin' those store shoes of his. That was one of the things about him was queer. He always wore store shoes, 'cause he couldn't get much work around town, and he didn't need to wear the sod-boots we all wore. But that was just one small thing. If he'd pass one of us by Naylor's or somewheres he'd kind of light up from the inside all over the outside of his face, and look real odd about raising his hand to say hello. So we'd kind of make it easier on him by just mumbling as we passed, looking down at the mud caked on our sod-shoes. At least it seemed like the right thing to do. I don't know.

We were all as startled as Fred when Mose said he was takin' up with Vivie. There wasn't no cause for Fred to get so all fired sore about Mose liking Vivie, even if Mose *was* part nigger. It could of been put to a stop right then if Fred had played his cards right. But no, he went and hollered something big and powerful when Mose walked in and said it.

I was in there that evening, and Mose walked right up to Fred in the store and told him right out, "Fred Shutt, I'm taking up with Vivie." And Fred bounced up like as if he'd had someone tell him his traps had snared a cougar. "Like Hell you are," he screamed, and it was easy to see Mose was shook up by it, 'cause Fred is a big man and he looks like the devil sometimes when he gets all mad, when he's got them big brown specs on.

Mose didn't know what to do so he just turned around and walked off, and we had to sit there for an hour and listen to Fred rave about how he was going to Jeffersonville and see the man there about the Klan, and whether wouldn't they come up and see what they could do, and about how he was going to strangle Mose with his own hands, and slap the living hell out of Vivie for even seeing a goddamned nigger.

We tried to tell Fred that only Mose's old man had been a nigger, and that he'd up and left Miz Oliver when she was big with Mose, but he didn't listen none to that. He was carrying on something fierce about goddamned crazy niggers touching his clean little girl.

Nobody mentioned Vivie going down by the skeet shoot all the time with the Hatfield boys or with Ervie Belman. Fred was in a nasty mood and didn't nobody want to say nothing against his Vivie at a time like that. Fred can be a devil sometimes.

We didn't hear nothing more about it till last night when Fred came in the store and sat down and wiped his forehead with his sleeve.

"I just done it," he said, and we all wondered what, cause we had just about forgotten what had happened with Mose. So we asked him what.

Fred looked white and kind of like he'd had someone punch him in the stomach so that all the energy had gone out of him, and he said, "I just hit my girl." And we just stared, cause we figured it was about time anyway, her loving up anyone she saw fit, even a nigger kid, and that givin' the town a bad name.

"I told her if she ever saw that Oliver again, I was goin' to beat the hell outen her, and she said, no, you can't ruin my life, and I got up from the table, so the stew spilled, and came round and slapped her. Hard. She was a-cryin' when I left. I don't know what I'm gonna do, but she ain't marryin' no sonofabitchin' black!" Fred was running on something large.

So we just shrugged our shoulders and wandered off, cause it ain't healthy to be around a man when he has a trouble like that.

Then the bait fisherman from up by Four Forks, the one that come through about ten o'clock on the way back home from the sites, came busting in and started hollering that there was a shooting and blood all over the place and didn't we even give a damn what was happenin' in our town and we'd better make tracks over to that house by the trap sites. The only house over that way was Fred Shutt's.

So we made it over and sure enough, there was Vivie Shutt, all stretched out, and bleeding like a sunfish hooked through the mouth. There was blood all over the place, like someone had dipped their hands in it and then flung it all out and over everything. It was in Vivie's hair, and it made the yellow all brown and sticky looking with it, so you wanted to be sick right there.

Fred started screaming and we knew who he'd thought done it, and we was pretty sure he was right cause there was bloody prints of shoes all around that room and they was of plain shoes, not sod-boots like everyone around there wore. And the only one wore store shoes like that all the time, not just on Saturday nights or Sundays was Mose Oliver. So there it was.

And now we knew Mose was back in there. Back where they say if you stay long enough you never come out, just turn to a frog or somethin'. They got all kinds of tales about them swamps. They talk about zombies and the quicksand and the swamp dust that get to men that have been alone too long, and all.

Why in hell did he have to get himself staked out in there?

There was a whole lot of us in flatboats getting ready to go on in there, with guns and baling hooks and the like, even the Hatfield twins and Ervie Belman and his old man, the drunker. They was all friends of Vivie and her old man, one way or another.

So we poled out into the muck and started down through the opening. We couldn't even see any prints or nothing, cause once you've walked over swamp mud, it closes over and don't leave a trace of nothing. You could lose a regiment of foot soldiers in there and they'd never be found again.

It was weird. Around these parts we avoid them swamps, they ain't so nice, but here we was, going in there with the call of all them odd birds slipping by over our heads and the squish-squish of the flat-bottoms poling along, and every once in a bit someone coughin' or snufflin' and everyone else turning around to look.

We split up after a while and I was in the boat with Fred and Ervie Belman and his old man, the drunker, who's another guy we avoids, and Algy Foss from the barber shop and one other guy, I think was Dave Dunn from over Four Forks way. We went up one of the little cleared branches of the big mud, and was poling out in pretty clear water for a while.

It's one of them weird places in the swamp. Clear water under the flat-bottom so's you can see right to the solid mud down 'neath, with the little shells and mosquito crawlers and everything lookin' like they was all together in a mirror, not some on top and some on the bottom the way they are. It's quiet in there, too, even the birds stayin' out near the fringes of the swamp.

And, of course, the snakes don't make no noise.

I could see how the swamp dust could get a man in there. They say that when you're all alone and ain't got no one for miles around, the stuff starts whispering around you and it gets in your ears and your eyes and makes you cry and it gets inside your head and drives you nuts just from loneliness. There was an old trapper used to bring out moccasin skins for shoes and pocketbooks and the like a few years back that was found like that. All bawling and broke up like.

It sure was quiet like in there.

Fred just sat up straight as a new struck pine shaft in the front of the flat-bottom, looking this way and that, back and forth, his head swivellin' on his neck like as if he was on scent. And nothin' but shadows and hangin' vines and creeper and the stink and quiet of the place, so that it made you think there was someone with a razor blade sliding it up and down across your backbone.

Then I saw Fred cock his head to one side and motion Davey Dunn to stop poling for a bit. And we slid along for a moment with nothing but the whump-whump of the blood in our ears, till Fred made a sign to pole over toward the little outcrop just set in the middle of the stream, peeking round the bend in the water. So he did and we saw Mose then.

I tried to stop Fred, but it happened all so whip-fast:

Mose was all hunched over on the bank, sitting with his knees pulled up close under his chin and his hands draped over the knees so's he's was looking at the fingers, and his head down on his knees, too, so that he looked like a scared kid. And he was crying and moanin' something weird, so that the noise was a kinda wail out there in all that big nothing of silence.

All I could hear was him coughing and catching his breath like, and gasping out, "They ain't nobody...all by myself...just a smile...she coulda told me she wasn't gonna marry me...all alone...all..."

Then I saw Mose jump, and I heard the snap of Fred's rifle at the same moment. N'then Ervie Belman and his old man and Fred and Algy Foss and everyone was pumping shots into Mose, and he was just as dead as he could be, and I guess I got forgotten or something in my head, because I took a couple shots at him too. But he just twitched a couple times when the bullets hit, like he was hamstrung and still kicking, then he pitched over good onto his face and slid down the bank into the water, raising a cloud of mud and mosquito wigglers offn' the bottom.

We piled him in the flat-bottom, after Fred had kicked him a couple times, and was takin' him back when Davey asked it:

"Why didn't he run off when he saw us? He was facin' us?"

And I thought, and, yeah, he *had* been facin' us, so why he hadn't run off deeper into the swamp, I don't know. Guess he was too busy cryin' and all. Now what would a man be sittin' in the middle of a swamp cryin' for?

Only thing I could think of was that swamp dust.

On the Garbage Front
by Harlison
January 1955

Terry scratched himself. He stepped into his dirty jeans, fastened his belt and looked around for a T-shirt. He saw one on the bureau, clean, white, neatly ironed, and almost inviting him to put it on.

"Stella! Stellahhhh!" he screamed, beating his chest, tearing a few handfuls of hair from the expanse.

A small, mousey woman came running into the room, her face screwed up into one of abject fear: "Y—yes, Terry?"

"Ha many times I gotta tellyata fix ma tee-shut befoh ya put it out heah?" He drew back a wide hand and smashed her twice, back-and-forth, across the face, leaving finger marks on her pale cheeks.

"I—I'm sorry, Terry. I'll fix it." She went over and picked up the T-shirt. "Like this, Terry?" she inquired digging her nails into the fabric, tearing it in three places.

He smiled, a soft, happy, collie-dog smile. "Yah, yah, dat's duh way I like it. Onee make it moh like dis..."

He grabbed it from her hands, ripping it down the back in a deep swath as he did. In his strong, muscled hands the T-shirt soon became a torn, crumpled, smudgey bit of cloth hardly fit for an animal.

"Dat's how it's duh best fowah me!" He was contented.

Stella smiled a contented wife smile. "Will you have time for a glass of beer and some waffles this morning, dear?" she inquired.

"Nuh, I godda go downada gahbagefront. They havin' uh shape-up dis monin' dat'll pick duh men fuh duh day. I wanna be onna job tuday." He slapped her once more, ringingly, and left, shrugging into a peeling leather windbreaker.

Knife-edged wind whipped around the knots of men standing on the open flat, the rows of refuse trucks behind them. From time to time one of the men would surreptitiously look over his shoulder at the trucks, hunger in his eyes.

A burly man with a garbage-hook slung over his shoulder came out of a shack at the field's edge. He cupped his hands and screamed, "Okay, youse guys! It's a shapeup!"

The stampede, leaving the older men lying, many of them, trampled in the slowing settling dust, stopped just short of the hairy-fisted supervisor. He had one hand in the bulging pocket of a Navy bluejacket, his fingers making rippling motions in the fabric, as though he were caressing something. "Here they are," he bellowed, whipping a full-hand from his pocket and casting all the little number tags out into the crowd.

They were assignment tags for the day. Anyone with a tag could ride the garbage-trucks. It wasn't a long job, but it paid well. Fifteen dollars a day and all you could eat.

They scrambled madly in the dust and dirt for the small tokens. Terry elbowed past a grizzled veteran, digging his arm into the man's stomach. He saw a tag and bent for it. A sharp kick in the seat of his jeans sent him sprawling.

Terry turned over in time to get a foot in his mouth. It wasn't at all tasty. He spat once, showering bits of Cat's Paw heel onto the ground. Suddenly he realized why the crowd in his immediate vicinity was trying to crush him to a runny pulp. He felt it under his pants. He was sitting on the tag!

Fighting free of the last remnants of the charge he staggered to the foreman and handed him the tag, getting his name written in the log for that day.

He was about to get his assignment when the Union Secretary came out of the little hut and walked over. He was dressed in a black cashmere coat and dark hat, several large diamonds and a gold cigarette-holder.

He said, "You ain't paid your dues this month, Terry. I don't think it'd be such a hot idea for you ta work tuday. Somadaboys might take it bad-like that you was workin' without payin' ya dues, when they have to." He signaled the gangboss to strike Terry's name from the roster for that day.

Terry was mad. Really mad. He stepped up close to the Union Secretary and pushed his face into the other's: "Lissen, Feeny, there's enuff gahbuge ta go 'roun' tuday an'—uh—an' I wanna wukk, unnastan'? Now, do you put my name back on 'at list or do I smash you kisser all ovah dis lot?"

Behind him Terry could hear the rest of the boys making a wide circle. He knew this was the REAL shape-up. This was the day the garbage-boys faced up to the crooked politics of the Union or went back to suffer the slings and arrows of outrageous refuse. He felt a glow of pride in himself.

He was the workers' champion!

"How do you boys feel about it?" asked Feeny, waving his gold cigarette holder in the direction of the crowd.

The boys mumbled and murmured among themselves for a moment, and then a fist shot out of the crowd and struck!

It hit Terry right in the left eye.

He stared amazed!

A foot erupted from the tangle of workmen and kicked him in the groin. He went down. That was the signal. They piled on him, beating, pummeling, smashing, shaking, rattling, rolling.

They turned away, leaving him lying there, clutching the bent disc of his work-tag.

A voice filtered back from the men mounting their trucks, heads held high, ready to go out to GET THAT GARBAGE!

"Damn trouble-maker. When's that Terry gonna learn we don't feel oppressed? Man, that cat's too hot on this movie business. Alla time reformin'! Reform, reform, reform. Allatime the same jazz. Whyn't he get onna new kick!"

And Terry lay there in the dust and filth, crying. Too humiliated and tired inside to even admire the fine new rips in his T-shirt.

Reminiscences

by Shep Tulley
January 1955

Once upon a time there was a little street urchin named Orfunt Annie, who had blank white circles in her head instead of eyeball. This may sound odd, but it isn't really, when you know that she had blank sockets too.

Orfunt Annie was a real professional-looking street urchin. She could urch with the best of them. In fact, people would pass by her as she lay in the gutter begging for pennies and say, "Will you just look at that child! Isn't she nauseating!"

But little Orfunt Annie didn't mind. Because she had a dream.

Down the street, around the corner and over three blocks in the window of Sacks Fifth, there was a most wondrous something!

One of Sacks fifths.

And little Annie saved and saved and saved and robbed smaller urchins, and picked pockets, for three years, just so she could go to Sacks and buy that fine imported fifth.

Finally, on a wintry Tuesday just after a wealthy man in a beaver coat had given her a few extra pennies, she took out her IBM and added the total all together. And lo...! She had enough for the fifth. Oh, joyous happiness!

So leaping and skipping, and tromping on everyone's toes, she raced down the street, around the corner, and three blocks over till she was across the street from staring at that big, beautiful fifth.

Annie could almost feel the warmth of that imported liquor sifting down across her palate. She shivered deliciously and prepared to cross the street.

Right about this time a Freuhauf trailer broke the light, streaked across the intersection, and ran her flat.

Cherchez le Message
1955

Karj Dandrea, extra-special secret agent of the Galactic Federation sat quite still as the banks of klieg lights burned down into his eyes.

From somewhere beyond their perimeter he could hear the words of the Supreme Commander, "The Redge are advancing on our system, Dandrea, and the only person who can save Terra and all its dependent colonies is—*you.*"

The last word struck Dandrea with power and clarity. Suddenly his shoulders sagged, for he felt the burden was too much. The Commander continued as though he had not noticed the change in Dandrea: "The message we are preparing to pour into you, under hypnosis, is the keystone. It could only be carried by one man—one man thoroughly trained to get through the Redge lines and hypnotically conditioned so the message cannot be dragged out even under mind-wrenching torture. Are you ready to undergo this treatment? It is more thorough than anything yet dreamed in the mind of man."

Dandrea's head bobbed momentarily. The lights flared.

When Karj came to, a headache was ripping the lining from behind his eyes, the fibers of his brain seemed to be aflame. He was facing the granite countenance of the Supreme Commander. They were in the spacious, paneled, war-buttoned office of the Leader. Both the Leader and the Supreme Commander faced him.

"It has been completely buried, Agent," said the Supreme Commander. "Not even total brainwashing can dredge it from you. This time we *shall* get through!" A wild light showed for a scant half-second in the depths of his eyes.

"You *know* your instructions?" questioned the Leader, knowing full well Dandrea knew them better than the face of his mother.

"Yes, sir. I am ready to go." Dandrea replied, pulse quickening,

"Then...*get through*!" cried the Leader, slamming the desk top with a quivering hand.

Dandrea was hurried through the tube to the General Outpost GHQ. Three months it had taken. His left arm was a useless stump, still occasionally bleeding where the Redge torture-experts had used a vibro-saw on it, his body was a wearied and near-broken thing.

His face was puffy and the acceleration of the tube-car brought a grimace of pain to his lips as the blue veins near the surface strove to break through the pasty flesh stretched taut over his bones.

The tube-car whined to a stop and the three men bundled him into a waiting stretcher—he screamed once in terrible pain as a bearer gripped him too tightly.

They hurried through the underground passages, stopping only occasionally to blurt out a clearing password to a hard-eyed guard with flame rifle at alert.

The door to the Supreme Outfield Commander's headquarters rose out of sheer rock at their approach and two space marines parted at a word from a stretcher-bearer. The door opened and an orderly ushered them into the SOC's presence.

He looked up as Dandrea's stretcher was carefully set down before his desk. His brow drew down as he surveyed the hulk that had once been a Special Agent.

"Tough trip, Agent," the Commander said, quietly.

"Not so bad, Sir," mouthed Dandrea around a face full of broken stumps that once were teeth. The Redge experts were thorough if nothing else.

"I've just been reading the report from the De-Hypnosis Lab, Agent," said the Commander, ticking his finger against the sheaf of papers. "Care to tell me about the trip through?"

Dandrea hesitated a moment: "Not much to tell. They got my ship as I broke through near Bartma IX in the Horsehead Nebula. Took me to their GHQ on Red and worked me over.

"I spent two months there and they tried everything on me: trickery, torture, narco-synthesis, post-hypno suggestion, plain everyday beating, threats, brainwashing—everything except bribery.

"But they couldn't get it loose. It was piled in too well. They were getting set to just put me out of my misery when I clubbed my guard and stole his car. I'll never know how I made it to the rocketport and off that Hell-planet. but I did and I got through." He subsided with a gasp, a thin trickle of yellowish blood streaming out of his mouth and down into the torn neck of his jacket.

He gasped and swallowed, painfully. "I got here and they de-hypnoed me. I went through a lot, I guess, but it was worth it. The enemy didn't get the message." His eyes glazed and he could hardly see the expression on the Commander's face.

"No," sighed the Commander, ripping up the report from the De-Hypno Lab. "I guess they didn't. Not that it did us much good. The clever fools buried it so deep that *we* can't get it out either."

A Walk Around the Block
January 1955

Nighttime in Yancey was a velvet cold thing. The night dropped out of the sky like soft-spun candy and draped itself about my shoulders.

I hunched over, shoved my hands deeper into my pockets—unconsciously gripping the ring of keys tighter—and kept walking.

My late evening constitutional or *else*, I muttered inside my head. Doctor's orders, doctor's orders. The monotony of the phrase was a depressant to my ego. Nothing is more odious than doing something pleasant that is unpleasant because you are forced to do it. If you get what I mean. What I mean is— Oh, just forget it. It doesn't really matter. Just verbalizing again.

Yancey stood out as an irregularly marked line of building tops in black against the light black of the night. Every fifteen feet or so the naked yellow unwink of a street lamp flared up the darkness for a moment, then faded into a back-there-behind-me of non-existence.

Boring. This whole constitutional.

But then, I conjectured, isn't everything basically boring? Isn't life itself merely a game that has been played and played and played again with unfailing sameness? There can be only one real ending for the game, and why we persist in taking a whirl at it when we're pre-destined to lose is beyond me. Which is what got me wondering about God and all. Why?

Why what? That's just *it*! Why a God? Berkeley contended (not too incorrectly I might assure you) that we are all figments of the imagination insofar as we exist. None of this "we are thoughts in the synapses of a greater god" routine, but that actually a thing didn't exist if we couldn't see it, etcetera, because it didn't exist in our frame of reference.

Now you can laugh like Hell at that, but just for the sheer kicks of it I decided I'd try out an extension of Berkeley's theory. Ah, ah, ah, don't quirk up the corners of your lips. If you were walking along the dull, deserted rim of the world on Farrell Street at three in the morning, you'd think of something stupid to do, too. You might break windows though. *I* was merely suppositioning. There *is* such a word—isn't there? At any rate, I decided I was going to will something out of existence.

I turned off Farrell onto Causeway Boulevard and stopped for a moment near the corner to light a cigarette, striking the match off the fire alarm box. The click of my heels as I resumed walking followed behind me like a flock of timid grasshoppers. What should I will out of existence? Right then I almost decided it was all poppycock for myself to be doing such childishness and nearly dropped the whole thing as a bad chain of thought. But for some unaccountable reason I persisted. I would will my street out of existence. Not the whole thing, you understand. Just the street and both sidewalks all the distance from Emery Road to Kensington Court, including fire plugs, street lights, gutters, grass peeping up through cement, and anything or anyone who happened to be on them at the time. Merciless, wasn't I?

Well it was more fun that fact when I suppositioned it. I cut through the empty lot that bordered the Causeway and Menlo Park Avenue and took up the stride once again. Here was I, the thought lit in my mind for an instant, a man only fifty-two years old, almost in my prime, and about to be cut down by a cardiac condition. I snickered, tossing my head. Tall enough, handsome enough—you'd be surprised how many barmaids give me the eye—and actually wealthy enough, though Lord knows those taxes will cut it to nothing if that Renmoro Steel proposition doesn't go through next week. Have to call Kemp in Chicago on that tomorrow. Make a note of it. Mmmm. And who am I to be making references to the Good Lord? Here I am trying to prove he doesn't exist. Oh well...

Now let's get right to it with a will. Concentrate. The street in front of your house does not exist. It is gone. Vanished. It never existed it does not exist it will never exist it is gone. Kaput! What is gone? Something that was in front of your house. But there is nothing in front of your house. (Now you're getting it—that's the proper attitude for willing things out of existence!) Something which never existed is no longer there where it never was. It is gone as completely as Angkor Wat. As completely as the Lost Tribes of Someone-or-other. Have to look that up one of these days. It is gone. Gone. Disappeared. Evaporated.

I was beginning to believe it myself now. I could picture the expanse, running right up to the edge of my front lawn, as a complete total nothing. Funny, but it was the first time in my life I had been able to imagine Nothing. You know how you concentrate everything you have, when you are a little kid, to try and imagine what's outside the universe. Try to imagine Nothing. I never could, till I tried to imagine that street gone. And it worked, it was a huge bottomless hole in the fiber of space that signified eternal and unchanging Nothing. It was a hole in space. It was black Black. I could see it in my mind's retina. Nothing.

I was almost to the corner of Menlo Park and Emery Road. Then it was a short walk step-on-a-crack-break-your-mother's-back to the expanse of Maple Avenue, my street, which ran into Kensington Court. Which in turn was perpendicular to Farrell. Once around the cold, chilly velvet dark block to satisfy some stupid doctor. Maple to Kensington to Farrell to the Causeway. Down the Causeway through the empty lot onto Menlo Park. Menlo Park to Emery Road and Emery half way up the block to my house. Except there was no street after Emery. Emery was a solid concrete and hardtop asphalt roadway with cars zip-zipping across it, but a black Absence after that where Maple should have been. I wasn't suppositioning, that was the way it was. There just wasn't any street there. And for good measure I lopped off the empty yard that was on the corner of Emery and where Maple used to be. It was right next door to my house and I'd never liked it. No one wanted to build on it. Uneven terrain or soft ground or somesuch ridiculousness.

I was coming to the corner of Emery Road. My feet hurt from the walk. The smoke from the cigarette went whipping away in the faint breeze and my foot caught momentarily in the cuff of my pant leg as I walked. How nice it would be to have no cars coughing up Maple. No pedestrians. No street. Just the cliff with the sea behind and below it, up to the edge of my lot behind my house, with Emery running off parallel with the cliff out of town. Quiet.

I turned the corner at Emery and took a step toward my house.

Now I'm not blaming Berkeley. He was theorizing a helluva long while before I was born. And I'm not blaming you fellows from the fire department because they aren't long enough, but goddam it, how do I get across that chasm to my house? I think I left the bathtub running!

Is Science Fiction Literature?
March 1955

We appear to have come of age. And in this maturity we are now faced with a problem that never confronted us before: how do we force the public to accept science fiction? And even more pertinent in many of our minds, "Do we want to?"

That last question would appear to have a number of facets. The foremost, it seems, is whether or not we have anything to offer the general reading public, and if we do, what is it, and if it's good enough for the run-of-the-buying-mill reader, why don't we retain it and savor it all the more in seclusion.

Somewhere along the way we've been told that power is in our hands; that science fiction is the greatest thing since the invention of thought. And you know, the funny part about it is that quite a few of you believe it. You've had it drummed into your dear little heads over and over by people like Horace Gold and Tony Boucher till you lift your nose when someone casually mentions he doesn't read science fiction.

Oh, for the bad old days when they tried to stuff you into a jacket with thongs when you muttered praise of stuff like rocketships! Now, all of a sudden, we've got amateurs walking up to us on the streets (though Lord knows we aren't such Final Authority as all that) spouting Riemann mathematics at us while we moan. "They took my bright, shiny toy away!"

Yes, there appears to be a mass advertising campaign afoot, under someone's direction, which purpose is solely to shove science fiction into the public eye. Much like a cinder.

Now, back to the point in question; do we have anything to offer the general public? Have we, for years and years, been clutching to our bosoms a truly important field of writing? In short, to sum up: Is Science Fiction literature?

That estimable publication, WEBSTER's NEW WORLD DICTIONARY, offering us many contradictory definitions of the word, says: LITERATURE, noun, all of such writings considered as having permanent value, excellence of form, great emotional effect, etc.

Is this our little baby? Is this our fledgeling but newly cast out into the cold, hard world of book reviewers and Arthur Koestler? Can this be the same stuff we used to read, that guys like "Doc" Smith assured us was all in fun?

When the Kinnison boys playfully went their ways, distorting space, vaporizing planets, did we contemplate that some day they would evolve into deep, philosophical vignettes, replete with psychosomatic motivations and Freudian action?

Hell, no! I state bluntly: Science Fiction is not yet literature! That it may some day be, I don't question. If Orwell and Huxley and Stapledon could come close, I'm certain that if not the present crop of pros, then advanced boys of a later era will drag STF up to that highly regarded position. But what have we now? What have we seen in the last ten years that approaches literature? Has there been any?

There will no doubt be some controversy on the forthcoming points, but I think I'm relatively safe in asserting that for all-around justification in applying the term "literature" to a science fiction book, the only ones to come forth have been penned within the past five years, which may or may not be an encouraging sign. In my opinion they are either an encouraging sign or an unprecedented fluke of chance.

To my way of thinking, the only three pieces of full-length fiction— which is, naturally, the only kind we can adequately judge—which unquestionably fall into the category of "literature" are Ted Sturgeon's recent MORE THAN HUMAN, Alfred Bester's THE DEMOLISHED MAN, and far away the best of them all, EARTH ABIDES by George R. Stewart, which has been acclaimed sufficiently so that further bravos on my part will not mean anything. I am discounting works such as NINETEEN EIGHTY-FOUR and BRAVE NEW WORLD for they and their phylum, were not specifically written as science fiction but as parables and lampoons of other cultures and politics. Three pieces of fiction out of the countless millions of words written per-annum since good Poppa Gernsback burped his imagination and upchucked the start of this whole mish-mosh!

Why is science fiction not literature, and how do I come to regard the three mentioned items in that class? Well, let's first define our terms. Literature is HUCKLEBERRY FINN, MAYOR OF CASTERBRIDGE, FROM HERE TO ETERNITY, and THE OLD MAN AND THE SEA. It is such, because it deals, in the main, not with a river, a house, an army post in war, or a huge fish, but because it deals with people. That's the secret! It's what separates science fiction from that inlet leading to the great sea in which the farthest island is "literature."

Essentially, literature must deal with emotions and the characters of its cast under stresses and unusual circumstances. Science fiction uses the gimmick. See the difference? In a science fiction story, your primary factor is not the effect on Jupiter Lil of the introduction of mechanical concubines, but a detailed explanation of the social, political, economic, and scientific aspects of said invention.

There are no Michael Henchards or Pruetts in the world of science fiction. Heinlein has come the closest to giving us people, but his stories are all too short and in the final analysis they too must be seen to be mere gambits for exploitation of some scientific gizmo.

I'm neither egotistical enough, nor foolish enough to think that any answer I offer might be the final or the correct one. In fact, I'm not sure there is an answer. If there isn't, sometime in the year 2000 some little fan will be saying the same things: science fiction is not yet literature.

SF must learn the hard way. It has come up that winding strait in the sea which leads to the island of literature rather rapidly, giving hope to the fact that it may some day become worthwhile fiction. It has spanned the years from "Master of the Asteroid" with its stick-figure heros and heroines, its shoddy plot, its top-heaviness of science, and brought us warmth and insight such as Ted Sturgeon portrays in MORE THAN HUMAN.

MORE THAN HUMAN, not to categorically praise it, falls into my class of great literature mainly because it prys into the guts of emotion, it deals, certainly, with science. A gestalt entity is certainly science enough for anyone—though of a different caliber than, say, Hal Clement's contraterrene matter.

Just of late, with Campbell marching in the forefront, the ranks of editors who want stories concentrating more on the mental sciences, not the physical, have swelled, bearing on the tide of its new-found preference of fumbling, backward, self-conscious form of writing much as early science fiction was. Thus, it may be fairly well stated, the place where the boat of science fiction will stop skirting the atolls of mere contemporary endeavor, and set sail for that farthest island is the time when self-identification and deep warmth of insight are not only necessary prerequisites for a good yarn, but are actually an integral factor, as necessary as a scientific gimmick.

The few modern attempts to place a story in a science fictional setting while hewing to the rather rigid line of mainstream fiction have shown us something. None of them—LIMBO, THE DEVIL'S ADVOCATE, ONE, etc.—have been overwhelming smash successes but each and every one of them has elicited some fascinating comments from the reviewers and recognizers of good books. Each has brought forth comments both brash and bizarre, outré and outrageous. They have shown that there is something hiding there that can be dug out, if the person with the proper grip on the shovel comes along. They have shown that no matter how many scientific can-openers or nylon-run-stoppers you interject into a story you will not get emotional impact and hence, literature.

People are the only hope of science fiction. Like the gentleman who, in the early 1900s, insisted firmly that everything inventable had been invented, I say, without reservations of course, that science fiction has just about worn out its stock in trade along the lines thus far explored. The new hope of the field lies not along lines of the physical, social, or mental sciences, though lord knows, there is enough still left there to work with, but in the area of self-exploration, "Man, see thyself!" Is there anything more fascinating under this—or any—sun? You've got to admit that no matter how clever your story may be, you've got to have people to work the parts of its machinery. There are few stories, if any, that come off with no human protagonist. This is simply because there is no great feeling of self-identification, a thing which must be exploited to extract the full measure of content from an incident.

There has never been a science fiction story depicting a runny-nosed urchin of the future, prowling the slums of a latterday New York. There has never been a science fiction story pointing up the ramifications of a mixed marriage in the future. There has never... Ah, but I could go on all day. "But," shouts some old-timer in the crowd, "this isn't the science fiction we knew. This writing takes itself too seriously, there just isn't any entertainment!" On the contrary, old-timer. There is more entertainment. What vicarionism you once extracted from flashing between suns you can now intensify by flashing between those suns with a person who picks his nose, who carries a picture of his wife and kids in a crumpled wallet in his hip pocket, who suffers from arthritis in the joints of his fingers, and who, like yourself, must even urinate once in a while.

Perhaps characters like Kim Kinnison will fade away, but then, fun though they were, they were a breed of never-never characters that one finds less and less mature and attractive as time progresses. Sure the new breed of hero will be fallible, but aren't we all?

People of the type exemplified by Heinlein's Harrisman will come to the forefront, and instead of phony motivations for conquering the Universe we'll see some truly formidable opponents for our hero, opponents who will be all the more terrifying because they'll be so commonplace in their drives. It is a good deal more logical to see a villain who wishes to vaporize Earth because he has an overdeveloped pyromaniac's emotions, than to see him crouching by his planetary detonation device twirling his moustache and cackling fiendishly about getting even with all stupid earthmen for laughing at his inventions.

We've matured. There is no place for such japery. Science fiction has become, somewhat over our dead bodies, a drawing-room conversation piece mentionable in polite societies. Now when George O. Smith goes to a cocktail party and mumbles low, "I write science fiction," the sweet young thing is liable to coo, "Oh, you do? Did you read Asimov's explanation of the thermonuclear principles involved in the transformation of two planetary economies in his latest book, what was the name of it again?"

Through the advent of the atomic era, flying saucers, Hollywood's recognition of SF, and a multitude of other factors that happened to have clicked into piece all at once, we're now a literary focal point. Certain things are expected of us and certain things are not within our power to grant. Science fiction is not a medium that lends itself too readily to the type of writing of, oh say, MOBY-DICK. It is a medium that contains inherent scope, but the point I'm trying to make is that scope is not what literature contains. Sure, GONE WITH THE WIND and SKYLARK OF SPACE are both epics laden down with extravaganza and scope, but there is a world of difference. Our scientist hero and his capitalist buddy, not to mention his two saccharine girl friends, are not even remotely in the same category with Scarlet O'Hara and Rhett Butler. GONE WITH THE WIND deals, with the effects on people, of incidents. The civil war marches triumphantly through the book but never manages to take the stage away from the characters, thus enhancing and putting added emphasis on itself. Diametrically opposed, is Doc Smith's world-spanning opus wherein the characters are merely the means to the end. The end being a guided tour to the heart of the galaxy.

All well and good to explore those alien worlds—this is what we read SF for but it just isn't literature. Literature is something else again. No matter how thin you cut it, you must deal with what and how people think. If we have something to offer the mainstream reader, it is our own little invention, science fiction. It isn't by any means great writing, nor is it everlasting writing. It is a guided tour into a world of fantasy that no other form of penmanship can produce. And let's not call it "great writing." Science fiction is many things to many men, but it is not a replacement for true literary values. If you call it such you are guilty of not only a grievous misrepresentation, but of doing much damage to the genre. For science fiction cannot adequately stack up with the mundane writings critics have chosen to call classic. If you call it such and it is then seen to fall short, the field suffers. Besides, you'd be a damned hypocrite.

Look at it this way: somewhere along the line, someone, let's say Tony Boucher, decided he wanted to sell more copies of *Fantasy & Science Fiction*. How to go about it? "Ah," says he to himself, "here is a gambit." We'll say science fiction has true literary quality and prove it by miming the *New Yorker*, et al., with psychological little pastiches that will make Martha Foley's eyeballs surge. So he did, and he managed to drag in a dunderhead of Clifton Fadiman's class, and away we went, one merry race which has lasted for five years now and changed the face of the field completely.

Now I'm not one for deep science in a STF year, but even I can see the ridiculousness of many writers. For they are writers, not science fiction men. They have nothing to say, but they say it marvelously well. This, as I see it, is the state of science fiction at the present time.

But let me sum up rather concisely: science fiction is basically a form of entertainment. To credit one with the other's attributes is fallacious and foolish. Science fiction, I think, stands at a very dangerous point in the ocean of the literary world. It can spring a leak at this stage—from people crediting it with things it just hasn't got—and sink with a gurgle, not with bang, or it can sail merrily on its way down the waters, to that farthest island of literature.

Hardcover

May 1955

It had been under the burned-out house. Richie was quite certain it was the last one. For all he knew it might have been the first one. But something singular, of that he was certain. It was the only one he had ever seen, and of that he was sure.

Book. The word was one of those scratched on privy walls and he knew it well. "Johnny reads books," the walls read, or "Alice does it reading a book," or if they disliked someone: "Bookworm Burris." So the word wasn't unknown to him.

Richie had been going through the rubble of the charred building, kicking aimlessly at clods of mud and the dirt streaked chips that had been furniture. He wished wildly for a miracle so that his goddam home would be smashed flat or something. That goddam father of his was just skirting the line of treason, and Richie was scared white thinking what might happen were the PeepToms to get wind of it. Richie was seriously considering turning his old man over to the Cartel Cops and getting a reward, as well as relieving the tension, when he kicked over the rotting boards and saw book.

It was book. It was last book. Richie knew it was last book because he got around. He was a member of the Sage Street Muckers and an Advance Guard of the 4th Section Regimental Knockabouts. He got around, and no one—absolutely *no* one—had ever mentioned seeing a book. Even though he was thirteen, Richie had experienced thrills and sins an earlier world never even knew existed.

Richie made sure no one saw him pick up book. He bent quickly, shoved it under his jumper, hauled himself over the fence at the end of the empty lot, scurried through a maze of alleys and came out on the hill overlooking the Tube House.

Just thirteen, but he knew the thrill of a forbidden possession. It was book and by Chrize he was gonna read it.

Back of the Tube House, where the commuter-tubes began their runs every half-hour, he snuggled down in the dirt of the hill and looked at book.

His world outside, back around the other side of the Tube House, would have been more than shocked had they seen Richie looking at book. They were rather strict these days about such things. Gang fights with glass hooks on the ends of a five foot pole. Okay. Seduction of the little girl with the bows in her hair as initiation to the TV Non-Virgin Club. Okay. Book. Uh-uh.

Too many people found other ways to think about the things they were supposed to think when they read book. Then it cost the Cartel more to put them back in line, which in turn got Government mad at Cartel, which made Cartel angry, and cut off the good things they could provide, like tv sets and jelly apples and scented kitchen cleanser, and all manner of wonderful—necessary—things.

So book was out.

But Richie had come up with book, and he was goddamned if he wasn't going to read it. Wait'll the next meeting of the Muckers. He'd rack 'em and swow 'em! Man, they'd plow when they eared his find. Man, he was a topboy with *this*. So Richie read book.

He opened the warped and matted cover and looked at the title. It made no sense to him. Such words were gibberish. But Richie was determined to indulge in what he knew to be a sin.

He bent his head, squinted his deep-hued eyes and ran dirty hands through dandruffed blond hair. The more he read, the more he was embroiled by the senselessness of the thing. What did this mean? What was a...*what* was it?

The boy closed the back cover of the book, having skipped much, but still following a twisting passage through the pages of the volume. There was no comprehension.

Ah, to hell with it! Even if he didn't know what the hell it was all about, still he had read it, and wait till the Muckers heard about this. Man, it was top-top secret, and if it got out there'd be real heaps to clean!

The Muckers met on a Wednesday night, and Richie had two hours of school three days a week, and Wednesday was one of them. So he was compelled to keep the news of his find in back of his eyes, tied up in a small sack in his mind, and wait.

The school was a big thing. It reared up in the center of Town and was hardly ever used. Tardiness and absenteeism were no longer evils, they were mainstays. But Richie got a large-charge out of going to that queero school to hear that zagnut of a teach ask them questions. Teach wasn't a bad sort even if he was a demoted PeepTom. They'd demoted him from Section A of the PeepToms for missing an ex-college prof that had lived right in his own house-block, and he'd missed him completely. So now teach was PeepTom of Town School, and Richie liked to listen to the jerko questions he popped.

So Richie always went to school. He was never tardy and never missed a day. He sat in the best seat, way in the corner at the back, and looked at the rest of the kids with their knives (carving the names of their clubs in the desktops) and their rubber-bands (stick a sliver of coke bottle glass in and shoot *that*, man, that's *real* cool!) and watched them carefully, till teach asked a question.

Oh, teach asked some whingers, he did. Like, "When was the last pre-Cartel government purged? Chollie?" And Chollie would answer in his squeaky voice, "Who the hell gives a muckin' damn, teach?" And teach would answer, "Very good, Chollie." Or he'd ask, "Who was the biggest traitor of pre-Cartel government? Herb?" And Herb would spit once at Jenny in the seat next to him and lisp, "Which-ya want, Jawge Washington or my old man? They got *him* in '85."

The schoolroom would rock with laughter and teach would snicker and say, "No, Washington will do. Thanks, Herb."

It was Wednesday and teach was up front with his earphones on, peeping for whispers that might give him a clue to something that might get him re-instated in Section A.

Then came the first question.

Richie wasn't listening. He was mulling over book. There hadn't been much in it he'd understood, but one phrase had stuck with him.

Teach asked, "Where is the capitol of our Great and Glorious Democracy located? Richie?"

Richie's mind muttered to itself. He said what was in his mind. He shouldn't have.

"'Twas Brilling, and the slithey toves, did gyre and gimble in the wabe..." Then he caught himself. "Uh, what the muck ya wanna know for, ya lost or somethin'?"

But the damage had been done. The class's collective necks were twisted and craned at him. Teach stood with his mouth open. "Very, uh, very good, Richie. Excuse me a moment students, I'll be right back." He bolted from the room, while Richie sat and sweated cold.

What had he said. What?

Ten minutes later they came in through the classroom door. The big men with the black suits, skin tight.

Richie leaped up on his seat, backing off it onto the floor, against the wall, "No, ferchrissakes; lemme alone."

They took him by the arms, above the elbow, and carried him from the room, kicking, screaming, muttering gibberish that the other students could not understand:

"You are old father William, the young man said..."

Pretty soon, even that faded down the tiled halls, and they went back to spitting at each other.

Detour
June 1955

High Klein Termor Jurgen chortled oddly. He rubbed his thumb across the bridge of his nose, eyes twinkling. "Let him go," he said to the Lord Chancellor, waving his other hand at the rapidly evaporating figure of the secret agent.

"What can he do now? Even though he *has* stolen the specifications of the teledapter, can he stop our Great Attack? Can he stop the might of fifty thousand massed armadas, prepared to pour through hyperspace and—" at this point his hand closed slowly, clawlike, in a crushing motion, "—snuff out the puny orb of Irdibar?" He chortled again.

The Lord Chancellor looked dubious: "But you don't seem to understand, Your Almighty Highest Eminence." He paused in trepidation, looking for a sign of disapproval on Jurgen's face. "This is the first machine of its kind ever conceived. This is a machine that will warp matter through space. We can send our Panzer Divisions through right onto Irdibar, and invade at once. They will stand no chance. But now..." He motioned feebly.

"Yes?" inquired the High Klein in amusement.

"*Now* they have the plans. They can make a copy. They *might* be able to stop us somewhere along the road once we invade. It might draw the war out for a few more hours."

His brow furrowed in concern.

"Poo-poo," deprecated the High Klein. "In two days we will be ready—so my generals inform me—to commence. What can they do in that time?"

Reluctantly the Lord Chancellor agreed, what *could* they do?

Naturally they had underestimated. The Irdibarians had the rough idea already, and the basic unit prepared. The secret plans brought back by the secret agent were the final key.

So when the conquerors came through Hyperspace, the Irdibarians had the sinister teledapter all ready.

It was so simple to follow the Invader's plans, put the other teledapter where the indestructible armada would come through, and, distressingly enough for the High Klein who was in the lead tank, warp them instantly out into the airless space between planets.

The Lord Chancellor didn't even have time to mutter, "I told you so."

HARLAN ELLSON has been characterized by *The New York Times Book Review* as having "the spellbinding quality of a great nonstop talker, with a cultural warehouse for a mind."

The Los Angeles Times suggested, "It's long past time for Harlan Ellison to be awarded the title: 20th century Lewis Carroll." And the *Washington Post Book World* said simply, "One of the great living American short story writers."

He has written or edited 118 books; more than 1700 stories, essays, articles, and newspaper columns; two dozen teleplays, for which he received the Writers Guild of America most outstanding teleplay award for solo work an unprecedented four times; and a dozen movies. *Publishers Weekly* called him "Highly Intellectual." (Ellison's response: "Who, Me?"). He won the Mystery Writers of America Edgar Allan Poe award twice, the Horror Writers Association Bram Stoker award six times (including The Lifetime Achievement Award in 1996), the Nebula award of the Science Fiction Writers of America five times (including the Grand Master Award), the Hugo Award 8 ½ times, and received the Silver Pen for Journalism from P.E.N. Not to mention the World Fantasy Award; the British Fantasy Award; the American Mystery Award; plus two Audie Awards and two Grammy nominations for Spoken Word recordings.

He created great fantasies for the 1985 CBS revival of *The Twilight Zone* (including Danny Kaye's final performance) and *The Outer Limits*; traveled with The Rolling Stones; marched with Martin Luther King from Selma to Montgomery; created roles for Buster Keaton, Wally Cox, Gloria Swanson, and nearly 100 other stars on *Burke's Law*; ran with a kid gang in Brooklyn's Red Hook to get background for his first novel; covered race riots in Chicago's "back of the yards" with the late James Baldwin; sang with, and dined with, Maurice Chevalier; once stood off the son of the Detroit Mafia kingpin with a Remington XP-100 pistol-rifle, while wearing nothing but a bath towel; sued Paramount and ABC-TV for plagiarism and won $337,000. His most recent legal victory, in protection of copyright against global Internet piracy of writers' work, in May of 2004—a four-year-long litigation against AOL et al.—has resulted in revolutionizing protection of creative properties on the web. (As promised, he has repaid hundreds of contributions [totaling $50,000] from the KICK Internet Piracy support fund.) But the bottom line, as voiced by *Booklist*, is this: "One thing for sure: the man can write."

He lived with his wife, Susan, inside The Lost Aztec Temple of Mars, in Los Angeles.

CHRONOLOGY OF BOOKS BY
HARLAN ELLISON®
1958 – 2019

SHORT STORY COLLECTIONS:

THE DEADLY STREETS [1958]

SEX GANG (as "Paul Merchant") [1959]

A TOUCH OF INFINITY [1960]

CHILDREN OF THE STREETS [1961]

GENTLEMAN JUNKIE
and Other Stories of the Hung-Up Generation [1961]

ELLISON WONDERLAND [1962/2015]

PAINGOD and Other Delusions [1965]

I HAVE NO MOUTH & I MUST SCREAM [1967]

FROM THE LAND OF FEAR [1967]

LOVE AIN'T NOTHING BUT SEX MISSPELLED [1968]

THE BEAST THAT SHOUTED LOVE
AT THE HEART OF THE WORLD [1969]

OVER THE EDGE [1970]

ALL THE SOUNDS OF FEAR (British publication only) [1973]

DE HELDEN VAN DE HIGHWAY (Dutch publication only) [1973]

APPROACHING OBLIVION [1974]

THE TIME OF THE EYE (British publication only) [1974]

DEATHBIRD STORIES [1975/2011]

NO DOORS, NO WINDOWS [1975]

HOE KAN IK SCHREEUWEN ZONDER MOND
(Dutch publication only) [1977]

STRANGE WINE [1978]

SHATTERDAY [1980]

STALKING THE NIGHTMARE [1982]

ANGRY CANDY [1988]

ENSAMVÄRK (Swedish publication only) [1992]

JOKES WITHOUT PUNCHLINES [1995]

ВСЕ ЗВУКИ СТРАХА (ALL FEARFUL SOUNDS)
(Unauthorized Russian publication only) [1997]

THE WORLDS OF HARLAN ELLISON
(Authorized Russian publication only) [1997]

SLIPPAGE: Precariously Poised, Previously Uncollected Stories [1997]

KOLETIS, KES KUULUTAS ARMASTUST MAAILMA SLIDAMES
(Estonian publication only) [1999]

LA MACHINE AUX YEUX BLEUS (French publication only) [2001]

TROUBLEMAKERS [2001]

PTAK ŚMIERCI (THE BEST OF HARLAN ELLISON)
(Polish publication only) [2003]

PULLING A TRAIN [2012]

GETTING IN THE WIND [2012]

PEBBLES FROM THE MOUNTAIN [2015]

CAN AND CAN'TANKEROUS (edited by Jason Davis) [2015]

COFFIN NAILS [2016]

NOVELS:

WEB OF THE CITY [1958]

THE SOUND OF A SCYTHE [1960]

SPIDER KISS [1961]

BLOOD'S A ROVER
(edited by Jason Davis) [2018]

SHORT NOVELS:

DOOMSMAN [1967]

ALL THE LIES THAT ARE
MY LIFE [1980]

RUN FOR THE STARS [1991]

MEFISTO IN ONYX [1993]

OMNIBUS VOLUMES:

THE FANTASIES OF
HARLAN ELLISON [1979]

DREAMS WITH SHARP TEETH [1991]

THE GLASS TEAT &
THE OTHER GLASS TEAT [2011]

RETROSPECTIVES:

ALONE AGAINST TOMORROW: A 10-Year Survey [1971]

THE ESSENTIAL ELLISON: A 35-Year Retrospective
(edited by Terry Dowling,
with Richard Delap & Gil Lamont) [1987]

THE ESSENTIAL ELLISON: A 50-Year Retrospective
(edited by Terry Dowling) [2001]

UNREPENTANT: A Celebration of the Writing of
Harlan Ellison (edited by Robert T. Garcia) [2010]

THE TOP OF THE VOLCANO:
The Award-Winning Stories of Harlan Ellison [2014]

COLLABORATIONS:

PARTNERS IN WONDER:
Collaborations with 14 Other Wild Talents [1971]

THE STARLOST: Phoenix Without Ashes
(with Edward Bryant) [1975]

MIND FIELDS: 33 Stories Inspired by the Art of Jacek Yerka [1994]

I HAVE NO MOUTH, AND I MUST SCREAM:
The Interactive CD-Rom
(Co-Designed with David Mullich and David Sears) [1995]

"REPENT, HARLEQUIN!" SAID THE TICKTOCKMAN
(rendered with paintings by Rick Berry) [1997]

2000ˣ (Host and Creative Consultant
of National Public Radio episodic series) [2000–2001]

HARLAN ELLISON'S MORTAL DREADS
(dramatized by Robert Armin) [2012]

THE HARLAN ELLISON DISCOVERY SERIES:

STORMTRACK by James Sutherland [1975]

AUTUMN ANGELS by Arthur Byron Cover [1975]

THE LIGHT AT THE END OF THE UNIVERSE
by Terry Carr [1976]

ISLANDS by Marta Randall [1976]

INVOLUTION OCEAN by Bruce Sterling [1978]

SCREENPLAYS & SUCHLIKE:

THE ILLUSTRATED HARLAN ELLISON
(edited by Byron Preiss) [1978]

HARLAN ELLISON'S MOVIE [1990]

I, ROBOT: The Illustrated Screenplay
(based on Isaac Asimov's story-cycle) [1994]

THE CITY ON THE EDGE OF FOREVER [1996]

MOTION PICTURE (DOCUMENTARY):

DREAMS WITH SHARP TEETH
(A Film About Harlan Ellison
produced and directed by Erik Nelson) [2009]

CHRONOLOGY OF BOOKS BY
HARLAN ELLISON®
1958 – 2019

GRAPHIC NOVELS:

DEMON WITH A GLASS HAND
(adaptation with Marshall Rogers) [1986]

NIGHT AND THE ENEMY
(adaptation with Ken Steacy) [1987]

VIC AND BLOOD: *The Chronicles/Continuing
Adventures of a Boy and His Dog*
(adaptation by Richard Corben) [1989/2003]

HARLAN ELLISON'S DREAM CORRIDOR,
Volumes One & Two [1996/2007]

PHOENIX WITHOUT ASHES [2010/2011]
(art by Alan Robinson and John K. Snyder III)

HARLAN ELLISON'S 7 AGAINST CHAOS
(art by Paul Chadwick and Ken Steacy) [2013]

THE CITY ON THE EDGE OF FOREVER:
The Original Teleplay (adaptation by Scott Tipton &
David Tipton, art by J.K. Woodward) [2014/2015]

BATMAN '66: *The Lost Episode* (adaptation by Len Wein,
art by Joe Prado and José García-López) [2014]

AUDIOBOOKS:

THE VOICE FROM THE EDGE: I HAVE NO MOUTH,
AND I MUST SCREAM (Vol. One) [1999]

THE VOICE FROM THE EDGE: MIDNIGHT
IN THE SUNKEN CATHEDRAL (Vol. Two) [2001]

RUN FOR THE STARS [2005]

THE VOICE FROM THE EDGE: PRETTY
MAGGIE MONEYEYES (Vol. Three) [2009]

THE VOICE FROM THE EDGE: THE DEATHBIRD
& OTHER STORIES (Vol. Four) [2011]

THE VOICE FROM THE EDGE: SHATTERDAY
& OTHER STORIES (Vol. Five) [2011]

ELLISON WONDERLAND [2015]

WEB AND THE CITY [2015]

SPIDER KISS [2015]

THE CITY ON THE EDGE OF FOREVER
(full-cast dramatization) [2016]

ON THE ROAD WITH HARLAN ELLISON:

ON THE ROAD WITH HARLAN ELLISON
(Vol. One) [1983/2001]

ON THE ROAD WITH HARLAN ELLISON (Vol. Two) [2004]

ON THE ROAD WITH HARLAN ELLISON (Vol. Three) [2007]

ON THE ROAD WITH HARLAN ELLISON (Vol. Four) [2011]

ON THE ROAD WITH HARLAN ELLISON:
His Last Big Con (Vol. Five) [2011]

ON THE ROAD WITH HARLAN ELLISON:
The Grand Master Edition (Vol. Six) [2012]

ON THE ROAD WITH HARLAN ELLISON (Vol. Seven) [2018]

THE WHITE WOLF SERIES:

EDGEWORKS 1: OVER THE EDGE & AN EDGE IN MY VOICE [1996]

EDGEWORKS 2: SPIDER KISS
& STALKING THE NIGHTMARE [1996]

EDGEWORKS 3: THE HARLAN ELLISON HORNBOOK
& HARLAN ELLISON'S MOVIE [1997]

EDGEWORKS 4: LOVE AIN'T NOTHING BUT SEX MISSPELLED &
THE BEAST THAT SHOUTED LOVE AT
THE HEART OF THE WORLD [1997]

AS EDITOR:

DANGEROUS VISIONS [1967/2002]

NIGHTSHADE & DAMNATIONS:
The Finest Stories of Gerald Kersh [1968]

AGAIN, DANGEROUS VISIONS [1972]

MEDEA: *Harlan's World* [1985]

JACQUES FUTRELLE'S
"THE THINKING MACHINE"
STORIES [2003]

NON-FICTION & ESSAYS:

MEMOS FROM PURGATORY [1961]

THE GLASS TEAT: *Essays of Opinion on Television* [1970]

THE OTHER GLASS TEAT: *Further Essays of
Opinion on Television* [1975]

THE BOOK OF ELLISON (edited by Andrew Porter) [1978]

SLEEPLESS NIGHTS IN THE PROCRUSTEAN BED
(edited by Marty Clark) [1984]

AN EDGE IN MY VOICE [1985]

HARLAN ELLISON'S WATCHING [1989]

THE HARLAN ELLISON HORNBOOK [1990]

BUGF#CK! *The Useless Wit & Wisdom of Harlan Ellison*
(edited by Arnie Fenner) [2011]

HARLAN ELLISON BOOKS PRESERVATION PROJECT

THE DIMENSIONS OF HARLAN ELLISON [2019]

THE EPHEMERAL ELLISON [2019]

THE ELLISON TREATMENT [2019]

THIS BOOK NEEDS NO INTRODUCTION
BY HARLAN ELLISON [2019]

EDGEWORKS ABBEY OFFERINGS
(Edited by Jason Davis):

BRAIN MOVIES: *The Original Teleplays of
Harlan Ellison* (Vol. One) [2011]

BRAIN MOVIES: *The Original Teleplays of
Harlan Ellison* (Vol. Two) [2011]

HARLAN 101: *Encountering Ellison* [2011]

THE SOUND OF A SCYTHE *and 3
Brilliant Novellas* [2011]

ROUGH BEASTS: *Seventeen Stories Written
Before I Got Up To Speed* [2012]

NONE OF THE ABOVE [2012]

BRAIN MOVIES: *The Original Teleplays of
Harlan Ellison* (Vol. Three) [2013]

BRAIN MOVIES: *The Original Teleplays of
Harlan Ellison* (Vol. Four) [2013]

BRAIN MOVIES: *The Original Teleplays of
Harlan Ellison* (Vol. Five) [2013]

HONORABLE WHOREDOM
AT A PENNY A WORD [2013]

AGAIN, HONORABLE WHOREDOM
AT A PENNY A WORD [2014]

BRAIN MOVIES: *The Original Teleplays of
Harlan Ellison* (Vol. Six) [2014]

HARLAN ELLISON'S ENDLESSLY WATCHING [2014]

8 IN 80 BY ELLISON (guest edited by Susan Ellison) [2014]

THE LAST PERSON TO MARRY A DUCK
LIVED 300 YEARS AGO [2016]

BRAIN MOVIES: *The Original Teleplays of
Harlan Ellison* (Vol. Seven) [2016]

BRAIN MOVIES: *The Original Teleplays of
Harlan Ellison* (Vol. Eight) [2019]

BRAIN MOVIES *Presents* BLOOD'S A ROVER [2019]

FOE: *Friends of Ellison* [2019]

WHY DO YOU CALL ME ISHMAEL WHEN
YOU KNOW MY NAME IS BERNIE? [2019]

The Harlan Ellison® Books Preservation Project was made possible by

Gary Wallen
Andrew Hackard
Jay Kemp
John Farmer
Stanley L. Korwin
Sven-Hendrik Magotsch
Dan Melin
Jay Corsetti
Eliot R. Weinstein
James Bocchinfuso
David Loftus
Stanford Maxwell Brown
William M Feero
William Dennehy
Mark L Cohen
Curt M Snyder
Rod Searcey
John Palagyi
Suzzii Barrafato, P. Stashio Nutz & Tortoni Spumoni & Co.
Dan McCormick
Andy Bustamante
Samantha A. Vitagliano
Mike Jacka
Alice Tatarian
David Jessup & family
Paul Guay & Susan S. Knight
J. Michael Straczynski
Raymond McCauley
David M. Barsky
Gordon H. Schnaper
Joel T. & Carole Hampton Cotter
Gerald R. Parham
Michael J. Dymond, MD
and 725 other Friends of Ellison.

Made in the USA
San Bernardino, CA
30 April 2019